DON'T DRINK THE WATER
A Citizen's Story

BOB McCORMICK
as told to Teresa Spencer

COLD RIVER STUDIO
NASHVILLE, TENNESSEE

Cold River Studio is an independent press committed to introducing fresh, exciting voices to the reading public. It is our mission to take a chance on deserving authors and achieve the highest quality when bringing their words to the marketplace. We believe in the power of words and ideas and strive to introduce readers to new, creative writers.

Published by Cold River Studio, Nashville, Tennessee

No part of this publication may be reproduced, stored in retrieval system, or transmitted in any form or by any means, electronic, mechanical, photocopying, recording, or otherwise, without written permission of the publisher.
www.coldriverstudio.com

First Edition: January 2011

All rights reserved.
Copyright © 2011 Bob McCormick
Cover Design © 2011 Cold River Studio

Printed in the United States of America
ISBN 978-0-9828146-7-3

To the Citizens of the United States of America

Introduction

Dear Reader,

No matter which nation we call home, which spiritual path we follow, or what our status in society is, it is time for us to stand together and call for a new approach to the global problems confronting our generation.

Imagine a time when a globally created judicial system allows us to settle all international disputes with our intelligence rather than our weaponry. Imagine a time when the concept of sustainability dominates our thinking about the environment. Imagine a time when the goal of eliminating poverty, hunger, illiteracy, and preventable diseases has become our reality.

That time is not an unattainable "Utopia"; it is the logical outcome of the ongoing evolution of human intelligence. We are not flawed. Cosmologically speaking, we are a very young species, and like every other living species, we are evolving. And now it is time to take the next step in the evolution of our intelligence. The book you're holding in your hands is not a work of fiction. It is not a dreamer's yarn, and it is not a theorist's conjecture. It is simply a tool for presenting a good idea whose time has come.

I am not the originator of this idea. It has been in the making for decades if not centuries, and it has passed through the hands and minds of leaders, thinkers, writers, and artists from all over the world. When I first came upon it, after decades of a life filled with both joy at the boundless potential of humanity and sorrow at the continual squandering of that potential, I understood that I would hold it in trust and pass it on to as many others as I possibly could. It is my hope that by the time you finish this book, you will have joined me as a trustee and champion of this idea.

When people hear or read the words "global government," they often balk. "I don't want to relinquish my rights and comforts," they might say. "I don't want to give up the life I know and love to be dictated by the culture, practices, and language of a world government that doesn't understand me or my values."

These are valid fears. And, luckily, they do not apply to the idea I am suggesting. The idea contained in these pages is not about achieving peace and sustainability through control. It is about wielding a far more powerful weapon: human intelligence. I am suggesting that *we call upon our national leaders to cooperate, as equals, in establishing a global cease-fire while we prepare for and hold a global summit where the topic is the long-term health of the entire human race.* Just as our leaders once gathered at the end of a devastating world war to establish the well-meaning, but unfortunately failing, United Nations . . . and just as our forefathers once gathered at the end of a hard-won war for independence to establish the unprecedentedly successful federation that we now prosper in, the United States of America . . . it is time again for us to lay down arms and work together to secure our future and that of our children.

I come to you as a fellow American citizen. I have no more intention of relinquishing my human sovereignty than you do. In the first eleven chapters of this book, I will tell you the story of how, over the course of my life, I came to believe that this idea is the best hope for all of us. I tell the story of my life here not because it is remarkable, but precisely because it is so unremarkable. Because it could be the story of any one of us. I share my story in the hopes that something in who I am resonates with something in who you are.

I have enjoyed that unique sense of community one feels when sharing a front porch with neighbors on a warm summer evening; I have played countless pick-up football games on the National Mall in Washington, DC; I have pushed my two children on a swing I hung from a black walnut tree in our backyard; and I have tried to do my best when it comes to service to my community. I love this country, and I love much about what it means to be an American. But my life in this country has taught me that there is much left to be discovered about being American and about being human—and I hope that in telling my story, I can share what I have discovered with you.

I hope, too, that in reading my story, you will see that I am not an idealist, a politician, someone with an ax to grind, a religious zealot, a revolutionary, or someone attempting to blame anyone else for the current state of human affairs. I am an "average" American citizen who has had the time and the desire to overcome the insecurity that comes with the cultural perception that an average American citizen has nothing to say about our nation's global and intergenerational responsibilities.

We, the citizens of the United States of America, find ourselves in a remarkable position today. Due to the efforts of our Founding Fathers, our nation is a government of, by, and for the people. Due to the efforts of past generations, we are in control of the world's only remaining superpower. Several times in the relatively brief history of our country, the world has turned to the citizens of the

United States for help. Our ancestors' selfless responses established our country as a beacon of hope for all humanity.

Today the human family is facing challenges unprecedented in our history. The very civilization our ancestors sacrificed so much to build is being threatened to its core by national and religiously justified killing, environmental destruction, and the accumulating effects of poverty, hunger, illiteracy, and deaths from preventable diseases. The rest of the world is in need of our help. We have the wealth, technology, know-how, and background to create a truly civilized society. But in the global arena, the American citizenry remains a sleeping giant.

Instead of leading the world in the development of a global judicial system that uses intelligence rather than weaponry to settle all international disputes, we have learned to accommodate a culture in which our national leaders are somehow agreeing, year after year, to spend more on our military than the combined military spending of every other nation of the world.

Instead of leading the world in the development of the technology necessary to create a globally sustainable relationship with our environment, we have learned to accommodate a culture in which our leaders act as if maintenance of our lifestyles is all we care about.

Instead of leading the world in the fight to eradicate poverty, hunger, and illiteracy . . . a fight that the UN estimates would only cost an additional annual expense of $62 billion to win . . . we have learned to accommodate a culture in which we spend in excess of 600 billion of our tax dollars annually on our military.

We have the potential to follow in the footsteps of past generations of American citizens and once again become a beacon of hope for the entire human family. Although this book is meant for and dedicated to US citizens, using the world's collective intelligence to establish and attain the long-term goals of humanity will require the cooperation of the citizens of every nation. But the responsibility of initiating the process falls heavily upon us, the citizens of the United States of America—and not on our leaders.

And this is why I write to you specifically—to my fellow American citizens. While the first eleven chapters of this book will focus on the lessons I've learned about our potential as American and world citizens, the final five will focus on where that potential can lead each and every one of us.

Where we are and where we've been are of little consequence compared to where we are going. The first step in any attempt to design an intelligent future for all humans is to have the wisdom and courage to stop defining and limiting ourselves by our past experiences. There are countless Americans who have recognized our unique position to be of service to the global community. And they are joined by governments, non-governmental organizations, spiritual and religious groups, and individual citizens throughout the globe who are working tirelessly and valiantly to make our world more livable—from small-scale efforts to distribute textbooks to impoverished schoolchildren to large-scale disarmament negotiations between rival nations. We are making progress. But we can all work smarter; we can be better organized; and we can succeed where once it seemed that at worst, failure was inevitable, or at best, success was somewhere off in the distant future.

We are facing global problems no prior generations have ever faced, and addressing our problems with the solutions of prior generations is not working and costing us precious time. Today humanity has a critical decision to make, for we are incapable of serving two masters. We can continue to pledge our allegiance and sacrifice our young to the institutions, beliefs, and organizations created by past generations, or we can pledge our allegiance to the long-term health of all future generations. We cannot do both.

The human story will continue to unfold. Political and religious foundations carefully set by past generations must be updated and revised with new thinking in order to adequately deal with our radically changing world. Looking back is not the answer and remaining where we are is unacceptable. The only question is, "Have we evolved to the point where we can intelligently design our collective future?" We won't know if we don't try. And what have we got to lose? Our risks are minimal compared to the possible reward: a workable plan for ourselves, our children, and all the generations yet to be born.

I hope you'll walk forward with me and others on the path we all share.

With hope and respect,

Bob McCormick
US Citizen and Founder of Globalsummit.org

Don't Drink the Water

Chapter One

*All truth passes through three stages. First, it is ridiculed.
Second, it is violently opposed.
Third, it is accepted as being self-evident.*
—Arthur Schopenhauer

I could still hear the sound of the tires on the gravel as Paul's pickup retreated down the drive. He was long gone; it had been minutes since his old Ford rounded the last visible bend and disappeared behind the trees, but I strained to listen until every last evidence of his visit faded. I could feel a hovering emptiness, shapeless and dark, waiting to move into the space Paul was leaving behind. I fought to stay with the sound. Was that the final crunch of gravel as he turned off the driveway? If I could have stopped the soft rush of blood in my ears, would I have heard his transmission kick in, would I know when he was accelerating onto the county road, winding through the woods and out toward the interstate, disappearing?

And then, suddenly, the sound was gone. I wasn't even aware of its last breath. One moment, I was leaning forward, hands gripping the porch rail, straining to hear. And the next—I was surrounded on all sides by silence, bone deep and still as stone. It was the heart of February; the leaves were down, and there wasn't so much as a rustling in the sharp, chill air. I was waiting for it; I knew it would come, but when it finally arrived, the silence was so sudden and harsh, so complete, that I felt caught off guard. As if provoked, as if blindsided after the whistle had blown.

Paul showed up at my door two days before in the way only a brother in spirit can. We grew up together, comrades on that precarious path from boyhood to manhood. We went to the same college as classmates and teammates, and we worked our first jobs together, wiling away long stockroom hours volleying crumpled paper cups back and forth between us. I was best man in both of his weddings; he was best man in both of mine. And when life gave to one and took from the other, we shared what we had.

So, when I found myself alone in a cabin in the woods, with nothing recognizable left of my former life and choking on the solitude I myself had created, it was Paul I called. I could hear the pain I'd tried to run from tapping at the door. Like a small army of shadowy creatures scratching at the edges of my consciousness, it insisted on gaining entry. When I understood that it was only a matter of time before the army beat down the door and surged up around me, I turned to Paul to stand with me, shoulders thrown against the jamb, holding it at bay just a few days more.

Paul never left upstate New York and lives there still. But when I called him from my cabin in the deep woods of Virginia hundreds of miles away, it was only a matter of hours before he showed up on my front porch. He stayed the weekend. There wasn't much to say. I was past the point of being able to give voice to a sadness I couldn't even understand myself, and with a friend like Paul, there was no need to. We sat on the front porch in the cold, letting a few words drift quietly back and forth between us. He couldn't save me from the wreckage of a battle I'd been waging in my own head for years. But with him there, I had one thin but sure thread to cling to, and it was possible to breathe in and out for those two days.

Life took over. At the end of the weekend, he had to get back to work. As I stood on the porch, watching him climb into his pickup and start the ignition, I could hear the army of shapeless creatures gathering at the door again, their nails scraping softly, persistently. I could imagine their long fingers closing around my lungs. I knew that the moment Paul was gone, I'd be left to hold the door closed against them on my own, and I didn't have the strength. Or the will.

I stood there listening hard enough to turn my ears inside out, cursing the years of construction work that had dulled my hearing. I listened as the last thread connecting me to the living ground steadily away through the gravel and faded to silence. And then I was alone. The moment the silence struck me, the creatures burst in.

In the sudden vacuum left by Paul's retreating wheels, I sucked the winter air in sharply through my teeth, felt it swell and roil in my lungs and then push back out of my throat in one soundless sob. With the next breath, my whole body was shaking. I gasped, trying to breathe as quickly as the sobs escaped, my chest thick with their pressure. Instinctively, I doubled over, wanting somehow to suppress the force crashing over me. I'd been here countless times before, consumed by uncontrollable tears, and always, they would run their course and leave me spent but relieved. This time, though, I sensed something was different. I could imagine no end to this jag; I recognized it as something beyond me.

Time retreated to the outermost edges of my consciousness. I wandered through the cabin, unable to see through the tears. It was all I could do to inhale between heaving sobs more like retches than breath. I was vaguely aware of sitting on the edge of a kitchen chair, my forehead in my hand. Then I was on the floor. Then on the bed, teetering close to the edge, my face in the pillow. I paced. I turned around the cabin furiously, half-trying to outrun the tears. I knew it was useless. I paced anyway.

I didn't notice the lengthening of the shadows until night had fallen. I realized with a start that I was in blackness, too complete to move about. I found a wall and sank down against it. I had known for months that it was a mistake to come to this place. What once seemed like a charming retreat, an escape from the persistent army that had been at my heels for years, was now a prison. I had longed for solitude, time to think, a reconnecting with simplicity, nature, what is fundamental. So, when I first stumbled on the cabin while out for an aimless country drive, I called the broker on an impulse. He told me that part of the movie *Clear and Present Danger* had been filmed in the cabin, and somehow that didn't strike me as being at odds with my vision of woodland calm. I moved in hardly three days later.

It was only then that I remembered the brutal murder scene shot where my couch now stood. And it was only then that I noticed the way the cabin's roof hung over the windows, blocking the sunlight. But I'd already hung heavy, forest green curtains over them and a dull, darkly woven tapestry above the fireplace. I didn't notice the lack of sunlight until I'd exacerbated it, unconsciously shutting myself into a permanent night.

I cried in the darkness. Sometimes my whole body was wracked with painful heaving and my ears rang with the strange, choked sound of my own voice. And sometimes the crying was barely a trickle. I shook soundlessly on the cabin floor, my body locked in a fragile trembling. I knew from the totality of the darkness that it must be night, but my body didn't react in any way. I felt no hunger; I did not sleep. There were only the tears.

Somewhere close to dawn, I found myself wandering out the front door and onto the porch. I didn't know what, if anything, drew me out of the cabin. Maybe I was trying to escape, maybe I hoped the splitting cold and the open sky would give me some relief from the weight of the sobs. Or maybe I had lost control entirely, giving over to purposeless steps that would lead where they would. Somehow I realized that I was standing outside, without a coat, in the semi-gray of early morning. I had cried through the night. Momentarily, the tears subsided enough for me to see out over the porch rail and into the dense trees.

Looking out through the naked branches, I could see down to the stream that ran along the base of the hillside where the cabin was built. It was a deep purple, almost black in the pre-dawn light, but still I could see its subtle shimmering. The stream had held me hostage countless times that winter. With every rain, it over-swelled its banks and flooded the drive, leaving me trapped in the accidental darkness of the cabin.

What a fool I was to come to this damned place, I thought yet again. There was no counting the times I'd had this thought since moving there. *What a fool.* What had I thought I'd find? Some kind of idyllic Walden? A reprieve from my mind, from the ever-lurking army of twisted, ugly creatures? Instead I'd only burrowed further into myself; I'd locked myself in.

And still I was crying. Through the cresting waves of pain that overwhelmed my consciousness again and again, a tiny, disconnected memory surfaced in my mind. *An old friend . . .* I couldn't think of his name or see his face clearly. *An old friend whom I used to head out to the woods with to camp. Sitting beside a fire with him, shooting the breeze, stirring the coals with sticks.* I remembered him looking into the flames and murmuring, "They say hypothermia's not a bad way to go."

I didn't know what triggered the memory; I wasn't even sure it was real. But I clung to it. "Not a bad way to go." Perhaps first my body would go numb. I imagined that would be painful—I knew the distinct ache of gloveless fingers on a bitter Buffalo morning. But after that initial pain? Perhaps there would be a quietness—a retreat. The real retreat I was looking for when I came here.

It would be pretty easy. In fact, I couldn't think of a simpler way to go. No weapon to buy, no need for hard-to-find prescription pills. No testing the rafters, no tugging on the rope to try its strength. I could just stroll down to the stream in my underwear, have a seat, and wait. I wouldn't have to watch my step. I wouldn't even have to stop crying.

For a moment, it seemed as if a tiny fissure was making its way through my tears. I felt a quick burst of cold fill my lungs as I took my first uninhibited breath in hours, maybe days. There *was* an end to this. Just a few steps away, an easy, painless, undramatic exit. No struggle. No clean up.

No clean up. As quickly as the fissure appeared, it sealed itself again. I was a father. I was a father, and I was a fool. There was no easy out. Yes, I could wander away and freeze to death and put a final stop to this mad chase. But in throwing off the pursuing army, I'd only be unleashing it on my children. No clean up? My son and daughter were grown, but I was still their father. The thought of gaining any relief at their expense was unendurable. I tamped it back down wherever it came from.

And then I was lost to the tears again. Pacing. Rising in and out of awareness. It occurred to me in a brief moment of lucidity that were anyone else there, the first thing he would of course ask would be, "Why are you crying?" And when I could only answer, "I don't know how to tell you," he'd have to conclude that I'd gone right out to lunch, that he'd stumbled on a loony in the woods and he'd better give him a wide berth. And could I disagree?

But worse yet, he might pat my shoulder and say, "It's obvious why you're crying." I was going through a divorce. I had moved away from Vienna, Virginia, where I'd lived for the last thirty years, where I'd become an active member of the community. I had a name and a reputation and what seemed in every respect to be the most I could ask for. And as my marriage and my place in the community receded further and further from my life, so too did many of my dearest friendships. Every way I once had of marking the passing of the days had gently fallen to the side, not all at once, but one by one, steadily, until what was left was a dark cabin in the woods, a lapse in real estate judgment that had come to represent the colossal missed mark of my life.

So if an old friend from Vienna were to have happened upon me then, he might have nodded knowingly and said, "Bob, of course you're crying. Anyone would cry. Take a sleeping pill, go to bed, and in the morning we'll find you a good shrink."

But he'd be wrong. I wasn't crying for my marriage. I wasn't crying for Vienna, Virginia, or for the committees I sat on, or for my career in local politics, or even for my many lost friendships. I was sure none of those losses did much to help my psychological state of affairs, but they were ultimately, sadly, beside the point. What got me to that cabin in the woods had little to do with any personal mistakes I made along the way, as great as those might have been and as devastating as I knew they were to so many people, not the least of whom were my wife and children.

The failure was much bigger than my single and—in the end—unoriginal story of personal struggle and loss. I failed at the one thing where failure was unimaginable, where its consequences were boundless and terrifying.

Over the course of my life, I had come to know with absolute certainty that a better path for humanity is possible, a path of cooperation, reason, and farsightedness, but I had been unable to communicate the idea. I understood that the line between what we call "primitive" and "modern" humans needs to be continually redrawn, and that our generation is standing on the wrong side of that line. We are all members of a generation that can still justify taking each other's lives, and we don't have a sustainable relationship with our own life-support system. Poverty, hunger, and illiteracy still plague our species with no end in sight. And thirty thousand of our children die every day from preventable causes.

I had also come to learn with the same level of certainty that we have the tools and the potential to intelligently create our own future, regardless of our current circumstances or our past experience. But the organization I founded to promote this certainty, the Global Plan Initiative, was stalling. The potential that I knew each of us holds in the palm of his or her hand—however large or small or privileged or impoverished that hand might be—threatened to go unrealized. And I had been unable to stir even those closest to me to recognize that potential, to open themselves to it, and to allow it to carry them forward. I had failed, and the consequences of that failure were too great to bear.

* * *

I cried for two days. I hadn't known it was possible for a human being to cry without pause for so long. I thought surely I would reach a point where I just dried out, but it never came.

Eventually, through the fog of my despair and panic, I understood that though suicide was out of the question, so, too, was continuing to endure the pain. I was headed over the edge. With no one left to turn to, and truly nothing left to lose, I called my wife.

We had not lived together for six months, and our marriage was effectively over. But she knew me, or at least knew the person I once was. She had witnessed my wrestling with the conflict between the problems that continue to confront humanity and the unrealized potential we have to overcome those problems. She had witnessed my despair when I first began to understand this conflict, and she had seen my joy and hope when I founded the Global Plan Initiative to confront it.

But she was also one of the many to whom I had been unable to communicate my thoughts effectively. She met my hope with resistance, telling me I'd bitten off more than I could chew, telling me to give it up. One day toward the end, as I tried to express to her the urgency of the idea, my hands dancing about with excitement as I spoke, she leaned back in her chair and said, "Bob, if you want to talk to me, you're going to have to stop using your hands." That's when I knew that she could not help me, and that if I wanted to continue, it would have to be alone.

Still, we had loved each other. When Paul was gone, when I'd cried alone through the night and knew the battle was all but lost, I called my wife. She told me, "Listen, I have a lunch appointment today. But I'll pick you up, and you can come along."

So I ended up at lunch with my soon-to-be ex-wife and our old friends from Vienna, a couple that I had been close with for many years before the Global Plan Initiative turned my life in a new direction. I managed to contain my tears through lunch. I sat there with red-rimmed eyes, unable to contribute, an empty husk. I'm sure they noticed my strangeness; how could they not?

I was leaking despair like a beached tanker. But they were old friends, dear friends, with a front row seat to the disintegration of my marriage. I imagined they wrote off my sorrow as regrettable, but all too common: a simple case of divorcé's blues.

My wife took me back to the house we had shared for all the years of our marriage. Immediately, the tears began again, and I found myself back on the couch in the living room. I had spent many nights there in the last two years before I moved out. And I spent that night there, too, hardly any different from the night of anxious wakefulness I'd spent in my darkened cabin. My wife, a lifelong nurse, gave me a sleeping pill, but the escape of sleep never came. I only cried.

In the morning, my wife's face appeared above mine through the blur of my tears.

"I don't know how to help you," she said. "This is beyond me. We're going to the hospital."

For another eight hours, I cried in the Emergency Room at Georgetown Hospital. They triaged the hell out of me. What do you do for a man whose ailment is weeping? They took my blood pressure. They started an IV, and I imagined the salt liquid shunting immediately back out of my tear ducts. They put me on a gurney and, bewildered, left me in the hall. As the third night of my crying began to fall, the on-call psychiatrist approached my gurney.

"Mr. McCormick," she said. "There's nothing we can do for you here. I recommend you check yourself into our Mental Health Care Inpatient Unit." She held my gaze. "It's a lockdown facility. Once you check yourself in, you'll have to stay until the doctors release you."

I nodded. What else was left to try?

I signed my name to the forms. I traded my shoes and their

contraband laces for paper slippers. And I walked through the heavy steel doors of the psychiatric ward.

The moment they locked behind me, the tears stopped.

Chapter Two

*We appeal as human beings to human beings:
Remember your humanity, and forget the rest.*
—Albert Einstein

I used to get these crying jags. From the time that I was a little boy, as far back as I can remember, until I was well into middle age—in fact, until not too terribly long ago. Every three or four months, I'd start to feel one coming on. I'd walk around in a funk for about a day, enveloped in deep blueness, knowing what was coming. And, sure enough, no matter what I did to cover it or squelch it or contort it into something else, the sadness would swell and swell until, inevitably, it would burst open, and for about fifteen minutes I'd cry like broken floodgates. Then, I'd dry my eyes, crawl out of my hiding place, and return to the world none the worse for wear.

The strangeness of this is not lost on me. A grown man, happy in his life and work, wanting for nothing—or at least nothing evident—sneaking away to cry without cause. Or, worse yet, a little boy growing up Catholic in South Buffalo in the 1950s, where the rules of living are clear and simple and where questions like "Why are you crying?" ought to have answers. As it turned out, there *was* an answer to this question, but I would not find it until much later in my life.

Until I did find it, I learned to be precise about predicting a jag. And I learned to hide. I didn't hide out of shame or dread. The truth is that these brief spells never really bothered me. Even if I couldn't explain them, I knew they would pass; I knew I'd come out of one relieved, so why bother with questions like "Why?" But while my tears weren't much of a problem for me, they were a serious problem for those who cared for me. In the regimented universe of South Buffalo, children had problems of one category—scraped knees, stolen pocket money, hurt feelings—and adults had solutions in kind—band-aids, a shiny penny, a kissed forehead. An inconsolable child, an *inexplicably* inconsolable child, turned the order of the universe on its head. And it was the helplessness in the adults' eyes when they found there was no remedy or even explanation that troubled me far more than the weeping itself ever could.

And so I discovered that in the stairwell of Saint Agatha's, the Catholic grammar school I attended until my family left South Buffalo, there was a pocket behind the door. The building was a simple, squat rectangle, with a church on the ground floor and two floors of classrooms above it. So that the children could pass quickly between classes, the stairwell door was always propped open, and where it met the adjacent wall, it created a little triangular nook just big enough for a nine-year-old boy to sit down and cry.

That's where I was one morning during fourth grade. I'd sensed a jag coming on as we filed in line from chapel back to class, and knowing the only alternative was to wail away in front of God, the nuns, and everyone, I slipped out of rank and made for the stairwell. This was usually an effective enough tactic; I could purge myself and get back to class before my absence became too conspicuous. But it was spring now. Sister Mary Francis, who taught my grade, had now had seven months for the oddity of my occasional quarter-hour "bathroom breaks" to sink in. And, if those weren't suspect enough in and of themselves, I was a talker.

I never intended to get in trouble. I got no pleasure or thrill from breaking the rules. But I couldn't contain myself; I came into the world having a good time, and even as a little boy, I was hell-bent on maintaining the trend. If there was a laugh to be had, how could anyone expect me to wait until Sister Mary Francis had finished chalking out the entire godforsaken multiplication table in agonizingly perfect right angles before I had it?

Sister Mary Francis was not the kind of woman to find precociousness cute. Not far into our notoriously troubled relationship, she leaned her sharp face close to mine, pursed her lips, and proclaimed, "You are the most arrogant child I have ever met."

I, never having heard the word "arrogant" in my life and delighted to find myself the focus of an adult's rapt attention, chirped a happy, "Thank you!"

It was all downhill from there.

So as safe as I thought I might be in my corner in the stairwell, I hadn't banked on the righteous thoroughness of Sister Mary Francis. When she discovered that I'd gone missing yet again, she combed the school for me, and soon enough, my muffled sniffles behind the door gave me up.

Sister Mary Francis was a rule-abiding woman, but she was not harsh. When her face appeared in the crack between the door and the wall and took in my huddled form, it softened immediately. But she could not help me. She, as much as any good citizen of Buffalo, had bought the direct line between cause and effect with religious conviction, and in her book, "crying child" was—had to be—a transparent problem.

She knelt on the floor beside me, and I braced for the inevitable: the unanswerable question.

"Bobby, why are you crying?"

I knew better than to tell the truth: "I don't know." At best, that would only get me that baffled deer-in-headlights look. At worst, it would land me back under Doc Houston's cold stethoscope.

And then—a flash of brilliance. *Lie. Conjure something out of thin air.* The crying was never the problem; it was the unanswerable question that was the problem. So, if I could answer it, no more problems!

I thought of the worst thing I could think of. I thought of the one thing I could that would answer the question completely, finally, so that I could get back to playing and laughing and breathing free from that incomprehensible adult need to comprehend.

"My mom and dad got in a fight last night," I told Sister Mary Francis. "And my dad got so upset that he banged his head against the wall." Her eyes widened. "And he got a concussion." I sealed the deal. "And now he's in the hospital."

I spent a few blissful hours thinking I was the cleverest boy on earth. Not only did I put a good tight seal on that bothersome question, I bought myself a tender pat on the head and a wide berth when it came to my talking. I walked home swinging my bag in an easy arc, wondering how long I could ride this new bubble of complicity between Sister Mary Francis and me.

And then I tossed open the front door of our little house to find my mother standing next to a massive bouquet of yellow daisies on the living room table, her brow crinkled forebodingly.

She gave me that look of perplexed exhaustion that could only mean trouble.

"Why do you suppose," she began wearily, as if bracing herself for certain shenanigans, "these flowers came this afternoon with a card that says, 'Mr. McCormick, We pray for your speedy recovery,' signed, 'The Teaching Staff of Saint Agatha's School'?"

I stood there flapping my jaw uselessly. My miraculous storytelling powers had, evidently, deserted me.

But perhaps that was for the best, because my mother hardly waited for a reply before she continued, "I called Sister Mary Francis with just that question. And she told me that she had the flowers sent to the hospital for your dear, unfortunate father, and that the deliveryman must have brought them over to our house when he found that Mr. McCormick had been released."

More useless jaw flapping. I could feel my heart clambering up toward my throat, as if desperate to jump this doomed ship.

"Go to your room," my mother said. "Wait until your father gets home."

I had known this was coming. This was the way of our household. My father was the patriarch, the enforcer, and my mother stood down on all matters of discipline. I retreated to my room to await the stick.

The stick and I were closely acquainted. Today, we would diagnose men like my father with alcoholism and recommend that they take anger-management classes. But in those days, my father was simply a hard-working, beer-drinking, big-handed construction man like any other, and he did what was necessary. He disciplined me as he himself had been disciplined by his own unsubtle Irish Catholic father. When certain behaviors needed correcting, he used the stick to prove his point. He never beat my sisters, one older and one younger than myself. This was the language of boys and men. And he never hit me with a closed fist. But otherwise, no holds were barred. I remember once he beat me seven days in a row, and the seventh—the greatest injustice my child's mind could fathom—was my birthday.

I knew when my mother sent me to my room that I was in for another run-in with the stick. What I did not anticipate was that my father saw this particular offense as calling for broader action. The lie, certainly, was one thing. I had shamed the family and inconvenienced the nuns, two egregious insults to the ordered South Buffalo universe. But the heart of the problem was the crying.

To a man like my father, there was only one worse fate than being a crybaby: having a crybaby for a son.

When he returned home, there was, of course, the requisite encounter with the stick. It was a dance we had both choreographed to perfection. We were both to position ourselves well clear of any obstruction. This rule came after the time my father, swinging the stick in a wide circle for greater velocity, had snapped it in two against the dresser. And I was to pull down my pants and lay across my father's knees, bare-bottomed. *This* rule came after the time I, aglow with my own resourcefulness, had slipped a spelling book in my underpants.

I don't remember the details of this particular beating. Whether I got more lashes than the usual, whether I cried more than before . . . the specifics have all slipped away, absorbed by what is now the general outline of a memory. When we walk the same path countless times, we don't remember countless walks, but a single one. So, too, with beatings.

I do remember what came next. I, thinking the worst was over, stood up and tugged my pants back on. I buckled my belt, careful to pull it high above the fresh welts on my backside. I wiped the snot and tears from my face with the back of my hand. And then I looked up to find my father still sitting on the edge of my bed, watching me with an intensity sharper than the stick itself.

"On Saturday morning," he said, "you'll get your real punishment."

Then he rose and disappeared into the hall, the door clicking closed behind him like a judge's final rap of the gavel.

Now, this I had not been prepared for. Up until that moment, the stick, though familiar, remained the most dreaded consequence conceivable, not only in my limited experience, but in my boundless imagination as well. That it could fall anything short of my real punishment left my skin cold and tender with dread. What could be worse than the stick? My mind seized on scraps of images from the school encyclopedia, stories I'd heard the neighborhood boys telling to impress each other. I saw medieval racks, an amateur Gettysburg amputation, the slow incessant drip of Chinese water torture. *What could be worse than the stick?*

I walked through the rest of the week in a burning haze of dread. Sister Mary Francis enjoyed an unexpected and total reprieve from my talking problem. My friends watched me with wary curiosity, sensing that I'd crossed into that threatening uncharted territory of "big trouble" and cautious of contagion. I stole the same wary glances at my father, both wanting and not wanting some clue into his plan for me, but our eyes never met.

On the day of reckoning, I waited in my bedroom for my father. This had been the scene of all other punishments, and it didn't occur to me that today would be any different. But this time when my father pushed open the door, he said only, "Come out here."

I found him waiting for me in the living room, holding a small, white bundle. My mother stood grimly at his elbow, and I wondered briefly if she knew what was in store. In retrospect, I'd like to believe she had no idea, but the truth is that even if she had had warning, she couldn't have been my ally. That was not the order of things in our home.

"Put this on," my father said, pushing the bundle at me. "Walk down to the corner, then turn around and come back again."

I looked down at the lump of cloth in my hands. It was a diaper and two safety pins.

My father had decided that the way to cure a crybaby was to treat him like one. He'd laid his plans carefully. He chose a Saturday morning to be sure that the most people would be out and about, chatting on porches, mowing lawns, watching their children play ball in the street. He gave his instructions with premeditated exactness: I would not be allowed to wriggle out of a single detail. I was to wear the diaper and nothing else. No shirt, no shoes, no socks. I was to clear the entire city block to the corner. No short cuts and no running. And he would stand watch on the porch to be sure I followed his instructions.

I did as I was told. I took off my clothes and put on the diaper. I walked out into the sunshine and crisp April air. I pointed my feet toward the end of the block and moved one ahead of the other, feeling my father's eyes at my back and the neighborhood's at my front. I made my way slowly to the stop sign; then I turned and walked home again. And I cried the whole time.

To this day, I will never know exactly which of my friends and neighbors saw me. I kept my eyes trained on my feet. But I knew from the hush that surrounded me as I walked that my father's calculating imagination had hit the mark. My tears had been called to account.

Somewhere between my first few steps and the interminable approach of the stop sign, a thought surfaced through my tears. *You're okay.*

I continued to cry; I continued to experience the shame and loathing of each step; I continued to be a nine-year-old boy walking up and down the street in a diaper. But somehow, at the very center of myself, I understood that this was only part of my reality. From the depths of my small body, a voice rose, less clear than my father's, but present nonetheless. *You're okay.*

It was of course years before I came to understand my father's fear and desperation. He was a construction man in South Buffalo with a crybaby on his hands, a problem that had to be wrenched in line by any means necessary, and he had exhausted his limited resources. I'm sure that if he could have had my tear ducts surgically removed, he would not have hesitated. He was convinced that I was in control of my crying—but I knew I wasn't.

But misguided as he may have been, he was only trying to fix the problem with the tools he had on hand. Like his carefully plotted shed, with each tool outlined in its place on the pegboard, he had a system for approaching the world. He saw no other alternative but chaos. This diaper, to him, was the next best solution.

And if it was a solution for my father, a means of closing a chapter, it was for me the first whisper of a possibility—a means of starting new, and boundless, chapters. As I made my way along the sidewalk, past the rows of houses and my hushed neighbors, I heard a voice within myself that was not my father's or my mother's or my friends' or the nuns' at Saint Agatha's. It was perhaps less clear, but it was just as strong. And it was saying, simply, "You're okay."

Chapter Three

When young people see that there are adults
who work to resolve conflicts peaceably,
they may be more hopeful about there being a future for them.
—Mary Finn, Kent State University

In 1960, without warning, my father got off my back. His letting up had nothing to do with sending his only son down the street in a diaper—innovative psychological warfare tactic though that may have been, all it accomplished was to teach me to be equally innovative with my hiding places. And less innovative with my storytelling.

No, what saved me had nothing to do with me. Instead, it was a surprise pinch hitter. Just before she began the fifth grade, my younger sister Paulette happened to take an IQ test that unveiled her genius.

The circumstances of the test are now lost to me. Perhaps she was part of a random sampling of students or perhaps she took it because my dad arranged it. What are *not* lost are the circumstances the test unleashed. My older sister Linda and I- who had taken no test and, as far as my father was concerned, had no need to after the family genius had been discovered—became instant afterthoughts.

I had no sense of my father's motivations at the time, but I now understand that he, just like any father, wanted to feel proud.

He wanted to have a special child. But as a boy, when I looked up at him, I saw him through the lens of awe that children wear for their parents. I saw a magnified man, larger than life, but his bigness indistinct and blurred. I could not make out what is obvious now, the knee-jerk defenses of a flawed and unsure man. I did not see the fiercely independent, self-taught young man who lost his dad when he was twelve. I did not see the youngest boy who watched from the sidelines as his oldest brother went to college on the only funds the family could raise. I did not see the Navy sailor who served as a master mechanic on the first submarine to enter the Sea of Japan because he wanted to come back dead or alive and nothing in between. I did not see an agile mind first mewed up then deadened by years of construction work, longing for any focal point. I felt only the dull weight of his large hand on my shoulder, pressing me at once forward and down. And then, suddenly, at twelve years old, I felt the hand gone.

I wonder today if I could have given Paulette fair warning. I had haplessly endured and eternally dashed my father's hopes since my first breath. Maybe if I had had the foresight to think beyond the immediate flood of relief and giddy freedom that came with that IQ test, I might have told her to look out for the diapers ahead. I might have been able to say, "Don't worry. This has nothing to do with you."

But I did not warn her; I only skipped blithely into an easy, open, American adolescence. I wrote for the high school paper; I was president of the Student Council; I played football; I was captain of the track team and king of the prom. I went steady with a girl whom all my friends agreed had won a looks lottery that I wouldn't even have qualified for. And through it all, my parents receded into the background of my life because Paulette had emerged at the foreground of theirs. Of all the football games I played and all the races I ran, my father never attended a single one. He was too busy guiding Paulette on his chosen path. He was going to have a doctor in the family. I remember the two of them sitting side by side at the kitchen table, gazing down at one of her remarkable report cards—six 100s and one 99—and my dad saying, "What's with the 99?" And I didn't warn her.

Then again, what good would it have done? The moment my father opened the envelope containing the results of that IQ test, a searing light went on in his mind that burned furiously for the rest of his life—and longer still. I imagine it is a light that will always burn for Paulette. Even if I had been able to see beyond myself, even if I had found the words to warn her, there would have been nothing I could have done to slow my father's relentless momentum.

Within days of discovering that he had fathered a genius, he was on the phone looking to enroll Paulette at Saint Rose of Lima, a feeder school for Holy Angels Academy, the most prestigious Catholic girls' high school in Buffalo. Of course, Holy Angels was still four years away for Paulette, but as far as my father was concerned, there was no such thing as over-preparation. Within a week, he had put a down payment on a house in North Buffalo close to the school. We were moving. When there's a genius in the family, everyone else steps in line behind her.

In my boy's imagination, the distance between South and North Buffalo was an intractable expanse. We were crossing the world, and I was lost at sea. Sure, I had been a bit of an odd duck on our block in South Buffalo. The sensitive, preoccupied kid who had an awkward habit of voicing every last thought, feeling, or curiosity. The vaguely eerie kid who happily talked to himself when no outside ear was available. The kinky-haired kid whose tight helmet of curls was all but alien in the whitewashed neighborhood. And finally—the diapered kid.

But it was still a neighborhood, that block on Remoleno Street in South Buffalo, and its inhabitants comprised an extended family bound by the particular, inimitable ethos of front-porch sitting. As a young member of the band of boys and girls calling themselves the Remoleno River Rats that played in the street and gathered on rainy days to rifle through the comics collected in an old appliance box on the Hammonds' front porch, I was an equal among equals. Odd duck or not, I had a place.

Then without warning, there I was, dunked with unstopped nose into the cold, foreign waters of North Buffalo. It was a friendly enough block, not that different on first glance from our home in South Buffalo. But second glance revealed a crucial, dampening difference: no front porches. Each house had only a small front step, just a place to retreat from the weather while fumbling through heavy coats for door keys. This almost negligible absence, little more than an architectural variation, rendered the block completely foreign to me. Something was missing. And though my father was too preoccupied with his new hopes, the rest of the family felt it, too—but we kept quiet about it. My homemaker mother, whose connection to the outside world had hinged on those front porches of South Buffalo, sank into a resigned, uncomplaining unhappiness. And I, for the first several months, teetered, unable to catch a foothold.

I did, however, have one advantage: the weightlessness of the release from my father's hand. I roamed my new haunts freely, and that's how I discovered the lifeblood of American boyhood. The paper route.

I heard from other boys at school that Buffalo's morning paper, the *Courier-Express*, could always use a paperboy, and I rushed home to ask my father for his permission. I got only an indifferent nod; my comings and goings were no longer cause for either suspicion or applause. He did not, however, neglect to garnish my wages by 50 percent.

What better retreat for the preoccupied kid with weird hair than an early morning paper route? I was out of the house by 5 a.m., my footprints always the first to crunch through the clean cover of new snow. In the muted silence of winter mornings, there would be times when I'd run the whole route, timing myself for speed and perfecting the neat arc of my toss. I racked up points for hitting the front step square in the center. In the summers, I learned to steer my bike at top speed with one hand, watching the paper glide with pristine geometry across the front lawns. And on Sundays, when the papers bulged with *Parade* magazine and innumerable ads, I reveled in the nascent strength of my arms as I pulled the loaded sled or wagon behind me. I became expert at judging the March mornings of half-melted snow: take the wagon and risk beaching in a snow drift, or endure the maddening scrape of the sled on bare patches of asphalt?

The athletic training was only the beginning. The real exertion of my paper route was mental. I was alone with the headlines, day after day, catching and releasing thirty times each morning the brightest and the darkest happenings of the ever-shrinking globe with my two child's hands. And I did not understand.

It seemed only natural to me that there should be some explanation for each headline, opaque as they were. So, into my private grappling with the news of the day, I invited the best debate partners I could conceive of. In my world, I had only two labels to apply to myself: "Catholic" and "American." And now that my father's influence had lifted, I had two remaining figures of authority: the pope and the president. Because in my imagination they could exist as whole and nuanced men instead of as the grainy, colorless images on the front page, I let them flourish, fully formed. I spoke with them out loud.

The debates first began in the fall of 1962, when, day after day, the headlines screamed with news of a crisis in Cuba. With each flick of my wrist and each arc of black and white sailing over the green lawns, the adult world loomed strangely in my mind. *If we fire first, they'll return fire. If they fire first, we'll return fire. Either way, we'll all be wiped out.*

By this time, I had taken serious training in what it meant to carry the labels "Catholic" and "American." The rule of "Thou shalt not kill" had been drilled into me in church and in school, and by age thirteen, I'd concluded that it was both reasonable and wise. I was prepared to follow it for the rest of my life. And now the headlines were announcing the possible demise of humanity, at the hands of humanity. My mind ricocheted back and forth between these incompatibilities. I was old enough to have a pretty good feeling for what the hell was going on when the headlines stamped *CRISIS* in black and white under my nose, and if I couldn't ask the authorities what it all meant in person, I did the next best thing.

"President Kennedy, it looks like everyone could die. What are you going to do?"

"We're negotiating, Bobby. But it's very complicated."

"Your Holiness, it looks like everyone could die. What can you do?"

"We're praying, Bobby. But it's very complicated."

I went round in circles. I seldom, if ever, understood the complications, but my source of questions was inexhaustible. My world had two supreme and ultimate authorities, two men whose stature partially filled the vacuum created by my father's withdrawal from my life. And yet—there were these headlines.

The logical explanation for them and response to them that I was looking for was beyond even the President of the United States and the Pope of the Catholic Church. The feeling of pent-up frustration those debates stirred inside my rib cage was not unlike the mounting sadness that preceded my crying jags—though I did not link the two at the time. Cyclical as my questions were, I asked and asked again. I wanted to understand.

When I had delivered to the last house on my route, I would inevitably have to table each stalemated debate. My consolation was that it would resume the next morning; there was never a newspaper that didn't provide more than enough fodder for discussion. And I had a haven for when the rising tide of impossible questions surged too high. Immediately after finishing the morning's deliveries, I would rush to the Carmelite Convent to serve as an altar boy at 6 a.m. mass.

The Carmelites are a cloistered order. At the right side of the altar where I assisted the priest in preparing the Eucharist was an iron grate, and behind that, a heavy curtain. Beyond the curtain, in a cool, dark place that I glimpsed only with my mind's eye was a choir of thirty nuns, singing hymns and Latin and Gregorian chants morning and night. They had given their lives to prayer, meditation, and song, and they sang with the flawless devotion of the sworn. These beautiful songs were made all the more haunting by the mystery that enshrouded the singers. The closest I came to seeing them was when I assisted the father in offering them communion through a small door behind the altar. It was my job to hold a gold saucer below each wafer as the priest passed it through the door, as a precaution against the Body of Christ slipping through aging fingers and falling toward the unclean floor. I was to monitor the wafer and only the wafer. I loved their voices, but I never saw the sisters' faces.

***

There *was* a single front porch on our block in North Buffalo. The surprising uniformity of the naked front doors kept me for a time from noticing the one exception to the rule, but shortly after I began my paper route, I spotted it. Across the street from our house and several doors down was, sure enough, a front porch. The porch hadn't come with the house; it was added. Just a concrete slab with a canvas awning and two chairs. And throughout the warm months, every afternoon, that one porch was populated by one man. He sat there like a transplant from my past life in South Buffalo, and so it was only natural that he became my first friend in North Buffalo.

I first spoke to him because I had to. The paperboys for the *Courier-Express* were responsible for collections, and so, in the evenings when subscribers were most likely to be home, I walked up and down the rows of houses knocking on doors and asking for payment. Eventually, because I was an incorrigible talker and because my neighbors were just as hungry for front porch ethos as human beings anywhere, I got to be pretty far behind in collections. It seemed as though every home I went to, I'd be greeted with, "Well, Bobby, glad you finally made it. Come in and sit down for a minute or two." Twenty minutes and a couple cookies later, I'd still be sitting in the same kitchen. It took me weeks to get through my list of subscribers just once. By the time I'd visited each house, I was already weeks late on the next cycle of collections.

In the beginning, though, I approached collections and knocking on each unknown door as most adolescents would—timidly. So, when I first walked up the driveway to greet Mr. Steinhelper on his front porch, I did it with trepidation.

On his lap was one of the small hunting beagles I'd eventually come to know well.

"Have you ever run with dogs?" he asked me.

I, of course, had not. He gestured at the metal lawn chair beside him.

"Have a seat," he said. "I'll tell you how. It's easily learned."

Mr. Steinhelper was seventy-two years old. This never struck me as remarkable—friendship between a thirteen-year-old boy and a seventy-two-year-old man. I simply fell into talking with him, because I was a paperboy who passed by often and because his presence on the front porch was for me a small kernel of familiarity so embedded in strangeness that I did not even know it as familiar. But, indeed, I felt at home on his front porch, and so it was where I went every day after school to sit and talk.

Until I met Mr. Steinhelper, easy conversation with an adult male was a complete unknown to me. My father was incapable of navigating the middle ground between domination and indifference, leaving me with only conjured popes and presidents to talk to. But now, on that front porch in North Buffalo, I was not without a friend. Mr. Steinhelper was an echo of that faint voice that I'd heard years before and that had shielded me from the brunt of my father's punishment. With Mr. Steinhelper, I knew I was okay.

Perhaps because of our difference in years, the usual dance of custom and courtesy was extraneous. To each other, we were just two people, without armor and without masks. We sat side by side under his green awning, the tubular metal chairs beneath us creaking, always talking, sharing our days' events and our thoughts about anything and everything. As our friendship progressed, it moved beyond the front porch to fishing on Lake Erie, running Mr. Steinhelper's hunting beagles in Grand Island, and skeet shooting. In the mornings before an excursion, I'd show up early, and we'd share a breakfast of fried eggs. He would take out his false teeth to eat and set them beside his plate; he'd chew with his mouth open, and it never occurred to me to flinch. He, in turn, never flinched at my oddness, never asked me to be any different than I was. Ours was a companionship of absolute safety.

Mr. Steinhelper was a skeet shooter, and after I'd spent a few Saturday mornings in his basement helping him load his shotgun shells with gunpowder and buckshot, he asked me if I would like to go with him on a skeet-shooting trip. He had a job for me.

My job was to load the clay pigeons into a machine. I'd retreat into a little wooden shed off to the side of the field, where the gunmen couldn't accidentally shoot me. I'd set the target into a mechanical arm, like a miniature catapult, and decide on a whim where to launch it. This random launch was meant to mimic the flight of a bird startled from its roost. Far outside my shed, each lone gunman would get set in turn, and when he was ready to fire, he'd call out, "Pull!" That was my signal. I'd release the machine's arm, and it would fling the clay pigeon out into the air like a Frisbee. Outside the shed, the gunman would sight the target and fire at it, the pop of his gun reverberating in the country air.

One day, after taking a few shots, Mr. Steinhelper made his way over to the shed and leaned his head inside.

"Ever shoot a gun before?" he asked.

"No, sir."

"Want to?"

"Sure."

"It's easily learned." He showed me how to point the gun and train my gaze to take aim. He showed me how to cradle it tightly against my shoulder and where to let my finger rest, lightly, against the trigger. I followed his instructions carefully, and when he was satisfied with my grip, I turned to walk out into the field, ready to take my turn at firing.

But Mr. Steinhelper caught my shoulder. "Now, just a moment, Bobby," he said. He looked me steadily in the eye. He was a big man, and though at thirteen I was sprouting steadily, he easily dwarfed me. He was always restrained, but never stern, and so I was alive with attention. I never took Mr. Steinhelper lightly, but I could sense that now, more than ever, was a time to listen up.

"A man crosses a threshold when he shoots a gun," Mr. Steinhelper said. Then he touched my shoulder lightly with one hand, and with the other, he motioned toward the field. "If you want to give it a try, go ahead," he said.

I walked out to the mark. I raised the gun and cocked it.

"Pull!"

The clay pigeon flew. I did my best to sight it, and I pulled the trigger. But I'd forgotten to hold the butt tightly against my shoulder. It rebounded violently, and I nearly lost my footing. The gun sprang free of my grip, and I fumbled with it, barely hanging on. A dull pain radiated outward from my shoulder, and my right ear rang with the sound of the discharge. Through the ringing, I could hear Mr. Steinhelper chuckling behind me.

He clapped me on the shoulder and grinned at me. Neither of us said a word about it, but an understanding passed between us in that moment. I'd go on to grow tall and strong in the coming years, with a quick coordination that served me well in football and track. Shooting a gun was the kind of thing young men like me were expected to be good at, but that morning, Mr. Steinhelper and I both knew it wasn't for me. I wasn't interested in living on the other side of the threshold.

That was the last shot I ever fired.

Chapter Four

Don't drink the water.
—Mr. Steinhelper

When I was growing up, my father and I were two travelers without a shared language, tossed together by chance in the same train compartment. We'd exaggerate our words and gesture broadly, and all we'd get in response was a blank stare, a shrug of the shoulders. We couldn't understand each other. And so we fell into silence, waiting mutely for the train to reach the station and let us out.

My poor father. He entered fatherhood with a certain set of expectations. He wanted a fit, strapping son who would excel physically and intellectually, who could both repeat his successes and finally realize his missed chances. Instead, he got a weird, sick child whose ailments and misbehavior seemed to lock him in a perpetual revolving door between the doctor's office and the principal's office. I presented my dad with a steady stream of interruptions to his plans for me. First it was chronic eczema that tormented my infancy and startled would-be admirers leaning over my baby carriage. Then it was night terrors that sent us back and forth to Doc Houston for sleeping remedies. Then it was the crying that persisted long past any normal boy's grace period. And, in the early years of my childhood, there was the dairy allergy that meant my father had to drive forty miles each way twice a week to buy me fresh goat's milk. I can picture him on those long, dull drives, drumming his fingers on the steering wheel, thinking how strangely things had turned out.

I know, then, that it was as much a relief to my father as it was to me when Paulette turned out to be a genius. He was glad to leave off dreaming up cures for my oddness that never seemed to stick. But he was still a man with a strict sense of order. Even though he was entirely done with placing any hopes in me after Paulette took her IQ test, he still fulfilled what he saw to be his fatherly duties toward me. And, for a man like him, a critical fatherly duty was to train a helper. He painted, sawed, hammered, reinforced, and sanded, and I helped. All my life, if I've run into anything that needed elbow grease, and if I had the right tool, I could work out how to do the job—and this I learned from my father. So it was that I grew up the family snow shoveler.

Our street in North Buffalo was laid out in neat stripes, like a patterned blanket. Two-foot-wide stripe of grass, seven-foot-wide stripe of driveway, house, grass, driveway, next house. Since my perennial winter chore was to clear the driveway of snow in time for my dad to park in the garage after work, this arrangement presented a particular problem for me. On mornings after a light snowfall, the job was simple: I could pile the snow on the narrow stripe of grass between our driveway and the neighbor's house. But as the winter wore on, the narrow stripe would reach its maximum capacity, and that's when the wicket got stickier. Then, I'd have to clear the driveway by first loading my shovel with as much snow as it and I could carry, then hauling it to the back or front yard, proximity being the deciding factor. Slowly, shovel full by shovel full, the driveway would inch toward passable.

Needless to say, this was not a charmer of a chore.

I had my methods for overcoming the drudgery of shoveling the driveway. I made up snow-shoveling games. And that's how, one day in the winter of my thirteenth year, my dad found me in the middle of admiring seven walls of snow that I'd laid out in neat rows running directly across the driveway.

Of course what I had done didn't make sense. I'd started shoveling normally, and as boredom—and thus creativity—overtook me, I switched to pushing the snow into horizontal barriers across the driveway. When a barrier got so heavy and high that I couldn't push more snow onto it, I'd climb over it and start another one. One by one, I'd made seven well-fortified walls. I knew I would eventually have to move my creations, but first I wanted to stand back and enjoy my handiwork. Bad timing.

I was so absorbed in admiration that I didn't notice my dad's truck until it was parked half in the driveway, half in the street, on the far side of my colony of walls. There they were, one three-foot-high behemoth after another, adding up to the absolute impossibility of anything, my father's go-anywhere pickup included, getting into the driveway.

My dad's face appeared through the window of his truck. As he looked out across the wholly blockaded driveway—the driveway he had asked me to unblock—his head dropped. I guess the thought that he was raising an idiot caused his neck muscles to give out.

And there, standing square in the middle of the driveway between two of the walls, clinging to his shovel and equally stymied, stood the wayward son. There was no explaining this one. I was just an odd kid.

* * *

Mr. Steinhelper gazed at me and shook his head. "Don't drink the water, Bobby," he murmured.

I blinked at him. This was not the answer I'd been looking for. The moment I'd finished, at my father's shouted behest, demolishing my snow walls, I'd beat a hasty retreat from home. I was overdue for a collections round for the *Courier-Express*. But more importantly, I needed an excuse to talk to Mr. Steinhelper.

And now here I was, sitting in his kitchen with a few cookies on a plate before me, and in response to my story, he was offering this little pearl of advice that might as well have been in Greek for all the sense it made.

"But—" I started, my hands waving uselessly in the air, the words catching and jumbled in my mind, "I can't seem to get anything right. How do I ever—" I was overwhelmed with not only the failure of having once again disappointed my father, but also the sinking feeling that I'd disappointed him without even intending to. How could I ever hope to do well when what came naturally to me was so at odds with what made sense to my dad—and, it seemed, most of the rest of the world?

"Don't drink the water," he repeated.

I dropped my hands and stared at him. He stared back, maddeningly calm.

"I don't know what you mean," I said finally.

Mr. Steinhelper leaned back against his kitchen chair. "Your dad wants you to swallow certain things about who you are and what you can do. You're going to find that lots of people want you to swallow their ideas about you and what you can accomplish." He shrugged. "So just don't drink the water."

I left Mr. Steinhelper's house just as confused as when I'd arrived. I had wanted him to tell me something clear, something I could act on. I had wanted him to say, "Here's the formula for pleasing your father. Do this, and you'll be on the right track." This mumbo-jumbo about water did not fit my plan.

But Mr. Steinhelper had a habit of being inconspicuously wise. I thought of him as my friend and—though I admired him—my equal in many ways. I might not have looked to him so easily for teaching if I'd known he was a teacher, and in retrospect I imagine he might not have taught so easily if *he'd* known he was a teacher. But he had a way of offering small darts of insight, sharp and to the point. I assimilated them without being aware of them. Only years or perhaps even decades later did I realize that my dad taught me how to do human things while Mr. Steinhelper taught me things about being human.

Most of the time, though, I did not go to Mr. Steinhelper for his wisdom or his experience. I hung out with him because he was fun. He was not an old sage on the mount, waiting for young pilgrims like me to trek through thin air for the benefit of sitting in his hallowed presence. He was just someone looking for a kindred spirit to spend time with, as was I. Very occasionally, very quietly, he'd offer me a rule for living that would sneak softly into permanent residence in my mind, but more often than not, we simply enjoyed each other's company, whether we were wiling away the time in conversations on the front porch or out testing the limits of our sportsmanship in the fishing boat or on the rabbit run.

As he promised me when we first met, Mr. Steinhelper taught me to run with dogs. He had two hunting beagles that were his pride and joy, and in the summertime, he would take them to Grand Island, not far from Buffalo, to compete. There was a clubhouse out there surrounded by acres of open field covered in tall grass and peppered with rabbit dens. When the season began, men would go out into the field and cut paths through the grass with lawnmowers. Then the beagle owners would converge to run their dogs.

The competition was simple. The owners would loose their beagles into the field to sniff out rabbits, and the dog that could pick up a rabbit's scent and stay on its trail the longest got the blue ribbon. The owners would know that a dog had caught a rabbit's trail because a beagle on the chase howls as it runs. The beagles couldn't be seen in the tall grass, and so, to be good and sure of which dog ran the best, each owner would set a runner who stood taller than the grass to chase his dog as it chased a rabbit. I was Mr. Steinhelper's runner.

I would run behind his beagle hollering, "Tally ho!" Anyone who has ever seen a rabbit run knows that it doesn't take off as the crow flies. It darts and weaves, changing directions to shake off its pursuer. And so, out at Grand Island, the beagles mimicked the rabbits' patterns. And I mimicked the beagles' patterns. I was never the fastest runner in the field, but I was agile, my reflexes were quick, and I could run forever. The rabbits and the dogs would tire before I did. I got to be so good that Mr. Steinhelper could rely on me to stay on his dogs' trail, and we won quite a few ribbons together. And not long after, when I went out for the football team in high school, I was one of the stronger players because of those runs. A runner that might have beaten me on the track would have a hard time catching me on the football field because I could turn on a dime when necessary. I never would have guessed it as a teenage boy sprinting through the tall grass with the wind in my face and the howl of dogs in my ears, but that skill would serve me well into middle age, winning me friends in college, keeping me out of a quagmire of a war, and even landing me a few jobs.

Memories like these overwhelm the space my adolescence holds in my mind. Sure, there is a place there for a scrawny kid clutching a snow shovel amidst a driveway of walls, always questioning his worth and unable to trust his own judgment. But these recollections take a backseat to others I can only describe as idyllic. When I think of the keystone of my youth, I do not see an overbearing father, shaking his head with disdain. I see Mr. Steinhelper sitting on the front porch, gesturing for me to take a seat.

Chapter Five

We are all students, and our teacher is life and time . . . Having earned good marks from our main teacher—life—we shall enter the twenty-first century well-prepared and sure that there will be further progress.
—Mikhail Gorbachev, *Perestroika*

Little by little, Mr. Steinhelper faded from my life. I was a teenager, engrossed in my steadily expanding world. I trusted that my old friend would always be there, a constant presence on that front porch a few doors down, but everything else was uncertain, always new, and begging for my attention. My days became crowded with sports, the student council, and a lovely new girlfriend who would end up becoming my wife. I stopped at Mr. Steinhelper's house on the walk home from school less and less often.

I doubt that Mr. Steinhelper begrudged me my absences. Whether or not it was preconceived on his part, he was the best kind of teacher: he worked to make himself unnecessary. He was only ever interested in helping me to understand that I was okay—and that my okayness came with my arrival in the world, just as everyone else's does. Slowly, subtly, he fed the kite more and more line until it was gone. When, at twenty-three, I heard from my mother that he had died, I still was not aware enough of his importance in my life to return to Buffalo for his funeral.

There was, too, another factor aside from the simple passage

45

of time that ultimately ended my contact with Mr. Steinhelper. Just as my father's decision to move the family to North Buffalo brought him into my life, my father's decision to move again ushered him out of it. In the summer after my senior year of high school, my dad issued the kind of left-handed decree that was his personal specialty. A distant relative of his died, and he got a good deal on her two-bedroom house in West Seneca, New York. Well, I didn't need to be a genius to tally bedrooms with family members. My older sister Linda was gone, so that left a room for Paulette, a room for my parents . . . and a clear message for me. It was time to move on.

This was the way my dad's side of the family communicated. My dad had learned the trick from his brother, who, when his oldest daughter finished her senior year of high school, bought a new dinette set for the family. He and his wife had three children, but the set he bought only included four chairs. The point was not lost on my cousin: her stake in the family home was being rescinded.

The trouble for my dad was that I didn't read the message quite as well as my cousin did. I planned to move out, sure. But I had no intention of doing what my father expected—getting a construction job and following the path that had more or less worked for him and that he figured ought to be good enough for his very odd son. I planned to go to college.

To my father, this was the kind of baffling idea that was right in line with building walls of snow across the driveway. As far as he was concerned, what use could I possibly have for college? I was not the family genius, but I had a good, strong back. A union job was waiting for me in construction, whether or not I had some silly calligraphy-coated piece of paper calling me a Bachelor of Something. Why spend thousands on calligraphy? Leave that to Paulette, who could actually make something of a degree.

But I was determined. Maybe it was those headlines I read over and over each morning, maybe it was Mr. Steinhelper's quiet influence, or maybe it was just my own intuition, but I sensed that there was a world beyond the regimented existence I'd come to know in Buffalo. And I knew that college could help me glimpse it. I wasn't sure what I'd do with a degree, but I wanted one badly enough to defy my father and to pay for it by working and borrowing.

So, when I finished high school and the family moved to West Seneca, I took my dad's hint and struck out on my own. But not toward a job in construction—instead, toward an education. Years later, when I graduated from college and held the diploma in my hand, my father would rewrite history. He would declare to my gathered relatives, "Bob didn't want to go to college. If it hadn't been for me, he would never have gone." And I would stand there staring at him, jaw unhinged in amazement.

Although I was perfectly willing and able to deviate from expectations when it came to going to college in the first place, it never occurred to me to stray from the standard when it came to *which* college I went to. I chose Canisius College, a Jesuit school in Buffalo, because that's where all Catholic boys from Buffalo went if they were accepted. I didn't even really think of it as a choice: Canisius had been the only possibility in my mind from the beginning. A secular school was out of the question, unheard of, and though I had the grades and the high school resume to get into a place like Notre Dame, leaving Buffalo had not yet begun to blossom in my mind as a potentiality. I made a tentative kink in my chains by enrolling at Canisius, but I wasn't ready to break them.

Within days of arriving at Canisius, I not only began to glimpse the world beyond Buffalo, I began to experience it all around me, in three dimensions, expanding outward faster than

I could ever hope to take in. All I had known my entire life were the unbending borders of Catholic Buffalo, a self-contained and self-assured planet where there was no conceivable authority outside the pope and the president and where after each mass we repeated a heartfelt prayer for the pagan babies in far-off lands like China. And now, here I was, among the comparatively tolerant Jesuits, who placed theology and philosophy at the heart of their curriculum and who set the thoughts of Plato, Hegel, and Nietzsche on the table for discussion. It was as if someone had suddenly thrown open the grating beside the altar so that I could see the nuns sing.

The classroom was where I first discovered, to my immense relief, that Mr. Steinhelper was not a fluke. That, in fact, the world was brimming with people ready to sit and talk and ask questions for curiosity's sake. But the classroom was only the beginning, and much of the learning I did at Canisius actually happened outside of class.

There were about twelve of us students who would sit around a large table in the cafeteria and lose ourselves in discussion for hours. We'd get a plate of hard rolls and a big pitcher of coffee and talk and talk until the coffee was gone and our classes were long over and forgotten. We had all kinds of different interests. There were psychology majors, economics majors, math and physics majors. And there were the jocks, the football players—myself and Paul, the same Paul who would one day become my last lifeline in a dark cabin in the woods. When he and I first took our places at the table and joined the discussions, we got some arched eyebrows. Jocks, interested in philosophical debates? But we proved ourselves. It was the kind of group that was self-selecting. Anyone was welcome, but those who got all the philosophy they wanted in the classroom weeded themselves out pretty quickly.

What we all shared was curiosity, a need to understand the contradictions that were cropping up all around us as we navigated the same wavering line from parochial childhoods to adult awareness of the world. By that time, many of us were grappling fiercely with belief. We'd all taken the same training growing up: as Catholics, we held the keys to the Pearly Gates. And now, we were discovering that different peoples all over the world each held their own sets of keys. Some of us dealt with this contradiction by tightening our grip on faith. Some of us, myself among them, dealt with it by gradually releasing our grip.

It was around that table in the cafeteria that I first began to get a handle on what Mr. Steinhelper had meant when he said, "Don't drink the water." I was beginning to leave behind a world of dogma and enter a world where distinctions could be made between fact and opinion. In my childhood, knowledge had only existed in truisms, and I was a believer. I learned rules like, "My country is the greatest, and my God is the only God." But now, suddenly, I was discovering that the world was indeed complicated—more complicated than I could have known as a young boy debating with the pope and the president. And I was also discovering that there were serious thinkers out there, in the past and the present, in my textbooks and at my cafeteria table, who were curious about the same complications that engaged me—and they were not accepting "It's very complicated" as a closing statement, either.

Those discussions taught me that it was possible for me to change long-held beliefs. I did not have to treat all knowledge as dogma. I could think things over and decide for myself what was fact and what was opinion. As Mr. Steinhelper had told me, I could simply decline to drink the water the culture was serving up. This was not automatic. It was difficult; it took time, and it was often disconcerting. But I learned that, the more knowledge I discovered, the more I could replace old thoughts—old ideas that I'd taken for granted without really examining closely—with new ones. I started to think of this process as *thought replacement*.

* * *

As much as I was evolving intellectually on those long days around the cafeteria table, I was no model student. Before I ever set foot on campus, I had decided that admissions tests were over for me. I had no intention of going on to law school or graduate school—the Canisius degree was all I wanted. I think I may still hold the Canisius record for earning straight Cs for all four years.

At Canisius, I was known as a "brown bagger," which meant that, in theory, I lived close enough to the college to be a day student and that I didn't need on-campus housing. But in practice, my family's house in West Seneca was not my home. My dad had gruffly muttered something about building a room over the garage when I asked him about my conspicuously absent bedroom, but this assurance had only ever materialized as a cot in the unfinished basement, curtained off by sheets I hung from the ceiling myself. More often than not, I just hung out and slept where I could—sometimes in West Seneca, sometimes in window wells on campus, and sometimes in sand traps on a public golf course near the school. I'd set myself up at the thirteenth or fourteenth hole, where I knew no golfers would arrive before the rising sun woke me up, and I'd form the sand into a little pillow. I was a happy and resourceful nomad for four years.

To support myself, I held a series of odd jobs, most at night and many with unsavory characters. For several weeks I worked at a freezer plant, an immense warehouse where frozen foods were stored. I'd spend nights pushing a dolly around the plant, stacking it with items for an order and then wheeling it out to the waiting truck. We were paid by the number of items we hauled from plant to truck, so once I'd finished unloading my dolly, I'd write down my total on a little pad. One day, as I was stacking the last of my boxes into the truck, Vick, a coworker of mine whom I often shot the breeze with and whom I thought of as a friend, walked up the ramp at the mouth of the truck.

"I'm taking four hundred pieces," he said.

"What?" I peered at him through the darkness inside the truck trailer.

"I'm writing down four hundred of the pieces you just loaded." I heard a soft scraping of metal and a moment later saw the glint of a switchblade in his hand. "Don't worry, you can keep the rest."

Without thinking, I threw my weight against the handle of my dolly. It sailed across the truck bed toward Vick. He had to spring backward off one side of the ramp to dodge it, and as he did, I bolted off the other side of the ramp. I ran all the way to the warehouse office and told my supervisor what had happened.

He shrugged. "That's between you and Vick," he said.

I picked up my paycheck the next week and never went back.

Schoolwork, then, was not a top priority. Between working, going to class, holding my own at the cafeteria table, and football, I had enough to juggle. My guidance counselor in high school had assumed I'd be a politician since I was president of the student council, and so he recommended that I major in political science. That seemed fine enough to me at the time, and as things turned out, it was a lucky pick. Most of my classes were graded based on a midterm and a final, which meant I really only had to show up for three weeks of class: the first week, to get a feel for the course and what was expected, the week of the midterm, and the week of the final. I lived through a few stressful weeks of cramming per semester, and the rest of the year, I enjoyed my own version of the college experience.

And I always managed to get that C grade. In one particular class, we all chose a country on the first day, and we were assigned to write a twenty-five-page term paper on its history over the course of the semester. I chose Spain, then promptly turned my attention back to our cafeteria discussions, work, and football. Three days before the paper was due, I went to the small Canisius library and discovered that I couldn't find much about Spanish history. So, not really thinking much of it, I sauntered over to my professor's office and asked him if he'd mind if I changed my country to England.

He gaped at me like I'd sprouted a second head and finally managed to stammer, "No. You'll write the paper on the country you chose three months ago."

Well, I wrote it. I went to the University of Buffalo library, scraped together some materials, and in three days I turned in a finished paper.

When the professor handed it back to me, there was my usual C in red ink at the top. But underneath was the note: "I would have given you a B, but I know how long it took you to write this." To me, then and now, his logic was flawed.

* * *

Throughout all four years at Canisius, I played football. The college had long ago dropped the sport as part of its athletics program, but there were several dozen of us who had played football in high school and who liked it enough to start a club team. We played because we loved to play. We hardly had any fans in the bleachers at our games, but that wasn't the point. On the football field, all I wanted was to catch the pass that looked like it couldn't be caught. I wasn't aware of time or place or even my own existence. I was only focus. All that existed was the ball, the movements of the players. And I wasn't too invested in winning or losing—it didn't matter to me whether it was practice or a game. I was a player playing. I would disappear out there.

It was on the football field that I first experienced the sensation of time in slow motion. It had never occurred to me that time could be experienced in different ways—that it is arbitrary; that in fact it is a human creation. And then, one day, my conscious perception of time shifted, if only for a brief instant. It was a real, physical sensation. In one suspended moment at the height of a game, I saw the ball poised in midair. I watched the other players moving at half-speed, as if in slow motion. Time had slowed, while I continued to move at speed. I remember the ease of darting through the lead-footed defenders and grabbing the slowly rotating ball out of the air.

As our cafeteria debates intensified and thought replacement was in full swing, I was growing more and more interested in logic, in describing the world in measurable ways, and this new addition to my experience of time was for me an interesting discovery.

And, perhaps most importantly of all, it was playing college ball that kept me out of Vietnam. During my freshman year, the club organized an exhibition game—ironically, the first tackle game that had been played at Canisius in over forty years—and I took a helmet in the knee just before half-time. I watched as the other player's head drove into my leg, and I heard a crunching, like tires on ice. We fell right by the sideline, and so I crawled easily off the field. But when I stood again, I couldn't find my footing. I felt like my left foot had slipped on a patch of ice. But when I looked down, there it was, on the ground beneath me, exactly as it should be. Why, then, was it not holding my weight?

I looked again. My left foot and calf were directly beneath me—it was my thigh that was out of place. It was sinking down beside my calf. My skin appeared to be the only thing holding everything together. I had to take hold of my thigh with both hands and pick it up, setting it down where my knee should have been.

I made my way to the bench. I found that if I didn't waver, I could manage a stiff-legged walk. When I sat down, the team physician took my leg in both her hands and felt up and down along the knee. She nodded.

"You should be able to play in the second half," she told me.

If growing up with my father hadn't sealed it, this certainly did—authority figures can be terribly wrong.

But, of course, I was still a very young man, and my judgment wasn't perfect. Paul told me he'd heard that knee injuries usually heal themselves, so I wrapped my knee in an Ace bandage, walked around campus as usual, and even managed to play a few games of touch football on it. Nature, however, had no patience for my stupidity, and soon enough my leg had swelled so hugely that I couldn't move it. I went to Mercy Hospital, and out of sheer luck, I was seen by Dr. Godfrey, who was at the time the head surgeon for the Buffalo Bills. When he unwrapped my leg and maneuvered my knee, his face actually lit up. He told me to wait where I was and disappeared from the exam room. A few minutes later he came back with several other staff doctors, who all bent over my knee in amazement. Apparently I'd suffered a very rare and fascinating injury.

Dr. Godfrey operated the next day. He warned me that I probably would never run again, but he hoped that I might at least walk. I didn't believe him; in fact, I completely ignored his assessment. As it turned out, not only did I run again, I went back to playing football, and I continued to play well into my forties. However, my left and right legs no longer looked like a matched set, and whenever I squatted down, my knee made an unnatural crunching sound. It didn't hurt, but it made its presence known.

And then, in my senior year, my number came up in the draft. Because of my March 26 birthday, I was number 63 out of 365 in the go-to-war lottery. For months, Vietnam had been all we talked about at our meetings in the cafeteria. Although the doubts we had about our religious upbringings varied, we unanimously and unequivocally subscribed to the rule of "Thou shalt not kill." Going into the military to learn how to kill other human beings would have been in complete opposition to our awakening minds. We agreed that whatever any individual chose to do to avoid the draft—whether it was to join the Reserves, which at that time let young men save face by enlisting but not enrolling, or to flee to Canada across the Peace Bridge connecting Buffalo with our northern neighbor—was justified.

At the same time, however, I had taken another very particular kind of training from my father and my uncles. Every one of them, with the exception of my uncle the priest, served in World War II. I simply could not conceive of telling them that I was heading to Canada. I knew I would be a terrible soldier, the kind who'd stand up in the middle of the field and shout out to enemy snipers, "Can we talk?" But ducking the rules of my country was not an option. When my number came up, I was certain that I would be going to war.

It did occur to me, however, to ask Dr. Godfrey for the records of my surgery. But he was a hawk. A staff person called me back and said Dr. Godfrey was sorry, but my records had been misplaced when they transferred offices. So I went to my physical with the Army empty-handed.

Everything went smoothly, as I knew it would. I was playing football on my healed leg; I had no reason to suspect that the Army doctor would take much note of my very minor limp. And, sure enough, he didn't. When he'd finished his exam, he clapped his hand on my shoulder and said, "Son, you're in fine physical condition. But tell me about that scar on your knee."

Convinced that nothing would come of it, I told him what had happened.

"Well then, one more thing," the doctor said. "I have to ask you to duck walk. Do you know how? Just squat down and walk from here to here."

I did as he asked, crouched down, and waddled for a short distance. Since my surgery, I had avoided doing anything to cause that awful grinding in my knee, and so this was quite possibly the first time I had squatted in four years. When I stood up again, the crunching sound was particularly loud. The doctor's face crumpled into a horrified wince at the sound. I, reacting to the doctor, winced too. The doctor, reacting to my wince, shook his head sympathetically.

"Don't worry, son," he said. "The Army doesn't want you."

I had seen the edge of the threshold Mr. Steinhelper pointed out to me when I was still a boy. His lesson had sunk into my core, and I understood what he did not need to say—that the ultimate threshold is not simply in firing the gun, but in raising it against and firing it at another human being. Whether I survived Vietnam or not, the life I've since come to enjoy would have been snuffed out by war. I would have come home forever changed. That football player who took out my left knee saved my life.

Chapter Six

The dogmas of the quiet past are inadequate to the stormy present.
We must think anew and act anew.
—Abraham Lincoln

Imagine a circus bear born in captivity. It has been trained to perform for crowds that come by its cage every day. It knows how, when commanded, to stand on its hind legs and roar, to balance on a little painted stool, and to jump through a hoop its trainer holds in the air. In return for its performances, it has a large, comfortable cage with grass to sleep on, fresh meals twice a day, and it is kept safe from any outside threat or intruder.

Perhaps this bear is one of several bears. Perhaps it lives in the cage with its mother, a brother, and a third bear that was captured from the wild not long ago and brought in to boost ticket sales. Four bears, after all, are better than three.

Now imagine the difference between the family of bears that has lived in the cage since they came into the world and the new bear, the bear that was born in the foothills of distant mountains, that learned from its wild mother to catch fish in a stream running through its territory, and that slept every night in the mouth of a shallow cave.

For the first bear, born in the cage to a mother that was also born in the cage, the cage is the world. Its mother and brother are the only other bears it knows, and jumping through hoops, waiting at the cage door for food to arrive mashed up in a tin bowl, and sleeping on a pile of dry grass are the only activities it knows. It is not aware that it is involved in an exchange of tricks for food; to the bear, this is simply the way the world works. Maybe, every once in awhile, it feels a little thrum of restlessness, an instinctual urge to splash in an open river or run through tall grass, but these drives baffle it. It has no context for them—the wild is more foreign to this bear than a man-made cage. And what's more, the bear's mother and brother live the same way it does. When it looks to them to see the right way to behave, it sees them performing tricks or sitting quietly by the cage bars. And so it follows their lead.

But the new bear knows better. It is depressed by the confines of the bars. It is confused by the commands of the trainer. And it knows the difference between performing tricks and roaming free along the mountainside. The wild bear knows its own bearness. The trained bear only glimpses its bearness on occasion, if it's lucky.

As a young man in Buffalo, I was a trained bear. In a sense, we are all trained bears. No matter what city or nation we're born in, no matter what historical era, we are all, inescapably, born into a prevailing culture. Maybe that culture is feudalism in twelfth-century England; maybe it's a culture defined by religious beliefs and practices; maybe it's a culture of fighting traffic on the interstate, trying to eke out an extra five minutes to stop by the coffee shop before rushing into work. This is a simple fact of being human, social creatures—we are all born in the captivity of an existing culture.

Our captivity is not automatically and exclusively negative. There are a lot of human beings on the planet, and every one of us, by nature, is social. We have to have mechanisms for organizing ourselves at various levels, and culture is the byproduct of those systems of organization. Likewise, the trained bear's life is not objectively bad. Its survival needs are being met. Maybe it even likes its training. Maybe it has some fun balancing on that little stool.

Trouble only arises for the trained bear when it starts to catch a whisper of its bearness. It might be a bear with unusually sharp instincts, wild urges that make the cage bars seems closer than they are or that suddenly, unexpectedly render the cold food in its dish unsatisfying. Or it might be that the presence of the new, wild bear awakens something within the trained bear—reminds it of something distant and indefinable. Somehow it begins to understand that the training it has always known doesn't have much to do with what it's really like to be a bear.

I can't describe how it happened, but somehow, when I was twenty-two years old, I suddenly no longer wanted to jump through hoops. From that moment on, I became more difficult to train.

The reality was that I had been performing very well. Within days of graduating from Canisius College, I had already scheduled a job interview with New York Telephone and a wedding with my high school sweetheart. By the end of July, I was employed and married. And there was absolutely nothing overtly wrong with my life. In fact, I had "made it." In terms of what my training had taught me to hope for and expect of myself, I was on top of the world.

I had my Canisius degree, which was quite a badge of honor as far as employers in Buffalo were concerned. And so I got a job in management at the phone company. Every day I put on a coat and tie, and I made a pretty good paycheck. But only seven or eight months into my stint there, the craft employees went on strike, and everyone in management was called upon to fill in for them. So I had to go out every day and repair telephones.

I loved it. From all the work I'd done with my father as a boy, I was able to get a handle on the technical side of the job fairly quickly, and the company provided me with a truck filled with every tool I could possibly need. Pretty soon I was going out on ten or twelve calls a day. I worked ten hours a day, seven days a week, for ten months. Needless to say, I made a lot of money—but that wasn't the greatest perk. What I loved the most was that, without my planning on it in any way, wherever I went, people were happy to see me. It felt like the old days, collecting for the newspaper. The strike had caused such a backlog in repair orders that by the time I showed up at people's homes, they had often been without telephone service for as long as two weeks. So, when I rang their doorbells, it was like I was Santa Claus paying them a surprise visit. This turned out to be a lesson I carried with me for the rest of my life: find a job where people are happy to see you when you show up for work. The hours were long, but I didn't mind.

It wasn't all smooth sailing, though. The work was demanding. I learned to climb telephone poles with hooks attached to my shoes. Now, I don't know for sure, but I imagine there are few places on earth colder than the top of a telephone pole in Buffalo in the dead of winter. And to make matters worse, you can't connect phone wires with gloves on. Once, I was at the top of a pole on a cold December morning, with sharp winds buffeting me the whole while, and by the time I finished, my legs had gotten so stiff from cold that I couldn't get down the pole again. But the cause of my predicament was also my bailout. Since I was at the top of a telephone pole, I had a ready line of communication right there. I didn't need to climb down to call for help.

I also had occasion to go into all kinds of homes, all over the city. I worked in wealthy neighborhoods, middle-class neighborhoods, and some really tough places. But everywhere I went, people were happy to greet me and chat as I worked. At one house, a woman had requested a service call because her phone wouldn't ring. At that time, telephones actually had two bells and a clapper between them that struck the bells when the current hit it. Her phone line was working fine, but the phone itself didn't ring. When I pulled off the plastic cover to find the problem, I unleashed hundreds of cockroaches that swarmed out from the phone and up my arms. The phone hadn't been ringing because it was completely stuffed with roaches.

These were the kinds of experiences that made the job fascinating. I counted myself lucky, as I had been at Canisius, to be getting to know the world and the people in it. And, just as I had at Canisius, I had a group to talk to. New York Telephone had a cafeteria, and before the strike, and again after the strike had run its course, a number of us would arrive about an hour early for work every day and sit around drinking coffee and talking. We didn't show up early to beat the commute—in Buffalo at that time, you could get anywhere you wanted to go in twenty minutes, whether it was rush hour or not. Instead, we got together in the same spirit that drew my neighbors in South Buffalo out onto their porches on warm days. We just liked to talk.

The difference, though, was that we didn't talk about ideas. We talked about day-to-day activities, like raising families or the ins and outs of work. At Canisius, we had been overwhelmed with input from the world of ideas, but at the phone company, our existence was fairly insular. All we experienced was work and home, and so that was all anyone needed to talk about. But for me, something was missing.

I began going around to my coworkers and asking them how they felt about their work and the company. I kept getting the same response: "The job is okay, but the benefits—especially the retirement benefits—are great." As a twenty-two-year-old staring down the barrel of at least a forty-year career, that wasn't the answer I was looking for.

And I was starting to get a sense of what it would mean to climb the corporate ladder. The man who hired me ended up becoming the CEO of one of the world's largest wireless networks. He was a good teacher, and he thought I was a good student. But the more I understood about the corporate world, the less it appealed to me. I had nothing against it, but it was a game I couldn't see myself playing—too many hoops.

I started to understand that what I was doing as an employee, whether I was climbing telephone poles or corporate ladders, was selling my time. And, to me, time meant thoughts. But when I was on the employer's clock, I was supposed to be thinking about things that served the company. So, essentially, I was selling my thought time for corporate interest. I began to chafe. I wanted to be in control of my thought time.

Then, just as I was beginning to experience this restlessness at the phone company, my wife started to talk about having children. For me, the timing was wrong. I knew, without even needing to spend a lot of time thinking about it, how I would step into the role of fatherhood. I would take it very seriously. I knew that when I had children, I would be a father first and foremost for the next twenty years, if not longer. And I knew that when I had children, I would stay put with them.

Somehow, I understood in my bones that I wasn't ready for that role. That's when I knew that I had no choice but to leave Buffalo. Something was drawing me away—I was beginning to sense the invisible bars of the cage.

But how could I ever explain this to my wonderful—and wholly innocent—new wife? She was the only woman I had ever dated. Because we had each other, we had floated easily over all the typical landmines of adolescence: dating, dancing, kissing, exploring. We were virgins when we married. And we were friends. We had every reason to believe we understood each other. So now, what could I tell her when she asked me, "Why are you leaving?" Instantly, I was the same small boy in the stairwell again, hearing the unanswerable question, "Why are you crying?" I knew I had to leave. But I could not explain why.

I honestly wished I could have told my wife, "There's another woman." That would have been a variation on our training that she could have understood. But the truth was that there was no simple key that would have clicked me back from dissatisfied to satisfied. It wasn't a matter of changing the color of my little painted stool or putting tastier food in my little tin bowl. I had to leave it all behind.

My family—including my father, who loved my wife and believed I never deserved her in the first place—was appalled. Besides, my dad was a product of the Depression, and he could not conceive of leaving a steady, paying job with absolutely no grievance. To him and to all of my family, the cage was fine. It *was* the world. So who the hell was I to shirk it? Where did I get off?

And they were not altogether wrong. There was much about my training that was positive, essential. I would not be leaving Buffalo empty-handed; I would be leaving with the ability to fix almost anything with the right tool. I would be leaving with the core set of values that my father and my Catholic educators had insisted upon. I would be leaving with the curiosity that Canisius had awakened in me. And I would be leaving with the personal confidence Mr. Steinhelper had helped me find. But that was all. The rest of the training became unnecessary baggage.

Leaving was a choice I made quickly, because it was the only conceivable choice I could make. But I did not make it carelessly. No one understood, and I had yet to find a way to give voice to what was for me a barely audible whisper. Worse still, my wife believed it was her fault. I was leaving the cage that was our home, I was no longer the person she loved, and I could not explain myself. How could she not be hurt? She believed that I was being cruel, and I had no rebuttal.

I did what I could to soften the blow for her. I left everything we had with her. Because I had been working long hours during the strike, we had over $10,000 in the bank—hardly small change in 1971. We had furniture and a brand new Chevy. I left it all with her. I took my clothes, $400, and the old car. And I drove away.

The moment I was on the highway, I knew exactly what Mr. Steinhelper had been talking about all along. I was no longer drinking the water. And I never felt so free.

Chapter Seven

For I dipt into the future,
  far as human eye could see,
Saw the Vision of the world,
  and all the wonder that would be; . . .
Till the war-drum throbb'd no longer,
  and the battle-flags were furl'd
In the Parliament of man,
  the Federation of the world.
  —Alfred Lord Tennyson, *Locksley Hall*

With Buffalo receding in my rearview mirror and a feeling of boundless possibility brimming in my chest, I set a course for Washington, DC.

I got behind the wheel without any plan. My only thought: to see and do things beyond the confines of the world I had known all my life—starting with that iconic expression of American freedom, the cross-country road trip. My friend Paul had moved to DC for a job after we graduated from Canisius, and he let me know about a party some friends of his were throwing down there. That party gave me a time and place to aim for. Beyond that, I figured I'd just drive away from Buffalo—and things would unfold as they would.

And so they did: there was a woman at that party. I arrived there twenty-two years old, separated, with nothing but $400 in my wallet and a goal to explore the United States. No sooner did I get started than I met a fellow explorer.

When she asked me if she could come with me on the road trip, I said sure—as long as she was able to buy a one-way flight home from any given city if things didn't work out. She agreed.

The catch was that her parents wanted to meet her would-be traveling companion. I went to their home, and they both drilled me. Their first questions, to my surprise, were, "Are you married?" and, "Do your parents know what you're doing?" They caught me off guard, so without thinking, I told them I was not married and my parents were aware of my plans. Both responses were untrue.

On the drive home, it hit me: I had just put myself right back in the same kind of cage that had driven me out of Buffalo. If I wasn't what they wanted me to be, and I pretended otherwise, I was once again performing tricks in a show that was not of my design.

I called them the next morning and asked to see them again. This time, I told them the whole story—that I was separated from my wife and that my parents had no idea what I was up to.

"I'm driving across the country. And if you're uncomfortable with your daughter coming along, then the three of you need to talk about it."

They did talk, and I assumed I would be right back where I started: traveling solo. But then they came back with a reply that nothing in my young upstate New Yorker's life could have prepared me for.

"We appreciate your honesty, and you both have our blessing."

And so I struck out across the United States with the woman I would fall in love with and who would become my second wife and the mother of my children. We traveled light and camped most of the time. When the car battery died, our resourcefulness grossly outstripped our funds, so we drove on without replacing it. Every day, we'd find some other driver to give us a jump. Somewhere in Tennessee, we made the ill-conceived decision to camp half a mile away from the highway. The next morning, we returned to the road and started flagging down cars and saying, "We need a jump. You can't see our car, but if you just drive down this dirt road . . ." It took us three days to find a willing Samaritan.

I learned that if I parked on a hill at the end of the day, when we returned to the car the next morning, I could just put it in neutral and start coasting. When the car hit about fifteen miles per hour, I could kick it into drive, and that would be enough to get it started. This was of course vastly preferable to waiting around for jumps, but when we got to San Francisco, the method posed a new challenge. The car couldn't get up to fifteen miles per hour within one city block. My uncomplaining companion and copilot would have to run down to the cross street and signal me to let me know when the coast was clear. Once I got rolling, there was no stopping for cross traffic.

We both liked San Francisco and figured maybe we'd stay—we knew by then that she wouldn't be needing that one-way ticket home. I started looking for a job, and one of the first ads I came across was for a "tree topper" at $25 an hour.

That kind of money was not to be ignored—whether or not I knew what a tree topper was. Besides, the name seemed self-explanatory enough, and I was sure I'd get the hang of it. In the past, I'd been able to talk my way into any number of odd jobs and fly by the seat of my pants. I'd built up enough confidence that if someone had told me they were looking for a brain surgeon, I might very well have volunteered my services. So I called the number in the ad.

The owner of the company asked me what kind of experience I had, and I answered, "Well, I've used a chain saw. And I climbed a lot of trees as a kid."

He hung up.

I would find out later that tree toppers in Northern California climb immense trees using thick belts and hooks, and as they climb, they saw off all the branches. The bottom branches can be as thick as their torsos. Tree topping is a huge undertaking—and saying, "I can do it," wasn't going to cut it this time.

That turned out to be as close as I came to getting a job in California, which is to say, not close at all. We decided to head back to Washington, DC. It didn't feel like a defeat, though; we were still moving wherever our whims took us, and there was something appealing about living near our nation's capital. So many of the debates that had consumed hours and days of my time at Canisius were related to the ideas and policies being discussed in Washington. To me, it was teeming water, alive and important, and I wanted to be on its banks.

But before I could settle anywhere, there were logistics to take care of. My future wife and I parted ways temporarily in St. Louis, and I went home to Buffalo to finalize my affairs there. In New York State, if a couple had no children and had been married for less than three years, they could get an annulment. My first wife had been able to obtain one without my even being there. The official summation of our brief union was that I had married her under false pretenses—I promised her children and refused to provide them. My uncle, Father Bob, who had married us, managed to secure for her an annulment from the Catholic Church as well. A church annulment was in no way important to me by then, but it was everything to my ex-wife.

I was relieved for her. And, perhaps too, for myself. I wanted to believe that I hadn't left her with any lasting scars. For some time, I continued to call her to check in on her until one day she answered the phone with a simple, resolute, "Don't ever call me again." I never did.

To this day, I do not regret leaving. But I do regret the impact my leaving—that relationship and others—had on the individuals who loved me, and who deserved explanations I was never able to give.

* * *

My cross-country road trip was finished, my life in Buffalo was officially, legally put to rest, and now it was time to build a new life for myself just outside the capital. We settled in Northern Virginia because it was cheaper than living in Washington, DC proper, and we started looking for friends and work.

As it turned out, I killed both birds with one stone. On Sunday mornings, I'd drive around Northern Virginia or the District, looking for guys playing football. Paul's job in town had run its course and he had returned to Buffalo, so I didn't know a soul besides my faithful road trip companion. But I wanted to play football. My only option was to scout out the parks or the National Mall to find a game. I always seemed to find one, and then I'd ask if they could use a player.

Naturally, I had to overcome some reluctance. Who was this unknown person butting in on their game or practice? They would squeeze me in sort of haphazardly, not wanting to be rude to a stranger.

And then I'd catch a few passes—and very quickly the reluctance would shift to openness.

"What's your name again?"

"By the way, where are you from?"

"Are you looking for a team?"

Some of the guys I met on the field are still my friends today. And more than once, they helped me find work.

When we first arrived in the area, I got a job as a forklift operator. Having learned my lesson after the tree topper embarrassment, I wasn't applying for jobs completely cold, and my experience did include operating a forklift on one of my warehouse jobs during college. So I started out as a non-union operator at $5 an hour. That was fine with me—I was in my early twenties, single, and living in a group house. Money wasn't a motivator.

But then I overheard that operating engineers in the union were making at least $12 an hour. Though I didn't need the pay bump to survive, and I wasn't looking to make any improvements on my standard of living, I did know that more money could mean less time working. If I had a bigger paycheck, I could afford to take more time off between jobs, and that was far more motivating to me than dollar signs. So I decided to do what I could to get into the union.

I went to the union hall in the District and told them I had a permit from Operating Engineers Local 17 in Buffalo, New York—my dad's union. All I remembered about it was the number, no names or details, and if they had handed me a written test about the equipment or operating procedures, the jig would have been up. I waited for them to ask for my credentials or to tell me to wait a moment while they called the union offices in Buffalo. I figured, "Take your shot in the dark, miss, and then go right back to doing okay at $5 an hour."

But they didn't call my bluff. At the time, the city of Washington was working on adding a subway system. Metro was a major new employer in the area, and there was a shortage of operating engineers as a result. The union officer asked me only one question.

"When was the last time you operated a compressor?"

I'd never operated a compressor, but that didn't matter. The question was absurd—an obvious formality. Compressors have two controls: *start* and *stop*. My answer? "About a year ago."

He handed me my union card. Just like that, I was a member of the DC Operating Engineers' Union.

The next morning, they sent me to my first union job—operating a backhoe. In a way, I'd lucked out. Back in Buffalo, I'd spent time working with my dad as an oiler on construction sites. An oiler is basically an operator's apprentice; before and after the workday, and during lunch breaks, he goes over all the moving parts of the machine, keeping them greased and checking that they're in working order. From those oiler jobs, I was just about as intimately acquainted with the mechanisms of most construction equipment as anyone, even if I'd never operated every machine myself.

As soon as I got to the site, I spent as long as I could sitting behind the backhoe controls, reminding myself which levers controlled which mechanisms. I was able to drive the thing passably well, but maneuvering the bucket wasn't quite as simple. Foot pedals controlled its side-to-side motion, while a hand lever controlled raising and lowering the boom. I was sure I could hold it steady—thus keeping the other workers safe from any errant swings of the bucket—but I wasn't so sure that I could dig with precision.

Before I had much of a chance to try maneuvering the bucket up and down, the foreman gave me my first task. There was a pipe that needed to be lifted out of a hole using the hook on the back of the backhoe's bucket. I drove the backhoe over and set the outriggers without giving myself away, but when I went to lift the pipe, I dropped the bucket and hit the pipe hard. Instantly, the two laborers leapt out of the hole, and understandably enough, they were furious. Since I wasn't touching the foot pedals that move the boom from side to side, I couldn't have hit either of them, but it was still painfully obvious that I was no master operator.

The backhoe was a rental, so the crew foreman called the owner, saying he needed a real operator. But my luck wasn't up—the owner turned out to be a pretty friendly guy, and, to my own amazement and relief, we hit it off. When he asked me what had happened with the backhoe, I told him simply that I was a little rusty. It had been a while between jobs.

"Well, I'll tell you what," he said. "I've got another piece of equipment called a pneumatractor. It's a lot like a backhoe, but the operation is simpler. You can get some practice on that."

A pneumatractor works exactly like a backhoe, but at the end of the hinged boom, instead of a bucket there's a giant jackhammer-like point used to break up concrete or tear down structures. Operating it is exactly like operating a backhoe, except that you don't have the added difficulty of maneuvering the bucket to scoop dirt. It's pretty hard to make a mistake on a pneumatractor—after all, the whole point is to break things up.

So, with a little practice on the pneumatractor, I taught myself to operate backhoes. And, at every job thereafter, I started taking my lunchtime—or any other spare moment—to get on other pieces of equipment and figure out how they worked. Soon enough, I was earning my $12 an hour as a pretty good operating engineer. And I had enough money to buy back a good chunk of thought time after each job.

***

One day, the tower crane operator on the job site didn't show up. The foreman was in a bind, and as a last-ditch effort, he asked if anyone on site could operate the crane.

"I can," I called out reflexively.

I had no more experience operating a tower crane than I had had operating a backhoe on that first day, but by now I had considerable experience with construction equipment. I knew for sure this time that if I jumped, I'd land on my feet.

A tower crane is a massive piece of equipment used in high-rise construction. It's shaped like a *T*, with a tall tower acting as the fulcrum for a boom that swings out above the project and is used to lift materials into place. The operator sits in a little cabin that hangs just below the juncture of the tower and boom, high above the ground.

It took me quite a while to climb up to the cabin. I sat down at the controls and discovered that, compared to other pieces of equipment I'd learned to run over the last several months, this one was easily the simplest. The controls were minimal: up, down, in, out, and swing.

If a tower crane operator can get to the point where the crane —immense as it is—becomes an extension of his own hand, he's as good an operator as any foreman could ask for. I got there quickly.

After that job, a buddy who played quarterback on one of my football teams and ran his own construction company called me up with an offer that floored me.

"They need an operator for the tower crane on the National Cathedral," he told me. "Are you interested?"

I was.

And so—almost overnight, it seemed—I found myself at what was to me the pinnacle of the construction business. Normally, a tower crane operator is constantly moving. From the moment he starts his climb up to the cabin to the moment he sets foot on the ground at the end of the day, he's working. His hands are always at the controls, lifting steel, pouring concrete . . . non-stop for eight or more hours. And if he's not good, the entire project falls behind schedule. By the end of the day, a good operator has definitely earned his keep.

Working on the National Cathedral was a different experience entirely. The whole cathedral is constructed from massive blocks of stone. My job was to lift one block, set it in place, and then lock off the crane and wait for forty-five minutes to an hour while the masons mortared it in. So I brought a lawn chair up with me, and I'd sit on top of the crane and look out over the city.

The National Cathedral sits atop the highest point in Washington, DC. And the tower crane stretched far above the highest stone in the cathedral. It was so high that I got paid an hour of overtime every day—a half hour to climb up and a half hour to climb down. As I looked down over the city from my lawn chair, I could see the dome of the Capitol and the Mall stretching out before it to the Lincoln Memorial. I could see the White House and the Pentagon. I could watch the traffic on Wisconsin Avenue; in the morning, bumper-to-bumper headed downtown, and in the evening, bumper-to-bumper headed to the suburbs. On the horizon, to the west was the state of Virginia; to the east was the state of Maryland. All of it stretched out under the crane, at once majestic and tiny.

I worked at the top of that crane for nine months. For nine months, the best possible view of DC was mine, and I had time to enjoy it. I never had a conscious epiphany up there. But every day, I looked down at the city that is the seat of tremendous power. I could see the places where decisions are made and at least two of the states where those decisions reverberate. And I could imagine those decisions continuing to reverberate even further outward, beyond the view from my tower crane, to all the states and throughout the world. What I could not see were the borders that separated those states and nations. Slowly, unconsciously, my tower crane experience helped me to see with my own eyes—before even understanding with my mind—that the world is not so big. And that the people in it, whether they are those who make decisions or those who experience the results of those decisions, are all connected and all look the same from atop the tower crane.

I wondered if all tower crane operators eventually come to the same conclusion.

Chapter Eight

In oneself lies the whole world and if you know how to look and learn, the door is there and the key is in your hand. Nobody on earth can give you either the key or the door to open, except yourself.
—J. Krishnamurti

My gig on top of the world didn't last. The National Cathedral project was funded entirely by private donations, and it kept running out of money. Every time they were out of funds, they'd have to stop work and let everyone go—with the exception of the stonemasons, who had come over from Italy. The rest of us, tower crane operators included, would have to pack up and either hope to find work elsewhere or wait until the National Cathedral organizers had built up enough reserve to call us back in.

In the past, spotty employment was okay with me; time off meant time to read and think. But then—everything changed. My traveling companion and I decided to get married.

My proposal was hardly one for the poets: "The last time I asked someone to marry me, I thought it would last forever. But if you're willing to give it a shot with the understanding that if it doesn't work out, that's okay, then I am, too."

And again—just as when, a few years earlier, she'd agreed to go cross-country with me with a one-way ticket home in her back pocket—she agreed. We married at twenty-five, and at twenty-eight, *both* of us were ready to start a family. The feeling I'd had six years before when my first wife had brought up the idea of having children was still with me: being a father would trump all other roles in my life for at least the next twenty years. Getting married and thinking about raising a family meant I needed more stable work than the on-again, off-again National Cathedral. But I knew that replicating my experience at the top of that tower crane would be impossible. I had scaled the Mount Everest of the construction business. It was time to move on.

Football once again came to my rescue. With the help of yet another quarterback friend, to whom I happened to mention my college degree, I found myself sitting in the office of a manager for New York Life. A life insurance company.

The outlook for me was not good. A major factor in getting the job was the size of your "Whom Do You Know?" book—the list of people you could count as contacts. Well, a tower crane operator doesn't make a lot of friends. My companions on the job were the clouds and the view, and though I'd made a few close friends playing football, I didn't really want to turn my teammates into insurance prospects.

There were two other guys in the interview with me—both of whom had grown up in the area. When the manager asked the first how many people were in his book, he said, "About 480." The guy sitting next to me said, "Between 250 and 275."

The manager turned to me. "How about you, Bob?" he asked.

"Twelve."

I walked out of there thinking that was the end of my chances for a job in the insurance industry. It turned out to be the beginning of a decades-long career. The manager called me up the next day and said that I'd have some legwork to do, but

I had impressed him in the interview, and if I wanted the job, it was mine. I may have left the city of Buffalo, but the state of New York seemed to keep tagging along: five years after leaving New York Telephone, I went to work for New York Life.

I had gone from being a free agent, responsible for no one but myself and living so cheaply that money was never an issue, to being a father. In a sense, after roaming the wilds, I had opted to return to the circus cage. But this time, I was entering the cage by choice, not by birth. I knew now that the cage is inevitable— no matter when we're born or where, we are born into a culture, and to survive, we follow its rules. The cages change with time and place, but there is no life—at least, no social, shared life— outside the cage. I was ready to go back inside.

Our son Ben was born in 1978, and Greta came two years later. The transition into adult responsibility was not easy for either my wife or me. I would wake up in the night with cold sweats, thinking about money. Three months after Ben was born, my wife, as we had planned, returned to work as a full-time nurse. But two weeks later, she came home crying.

"I can't be a nurse, a wife, and a mother," she said.

"Then you should quit," I answered.

Much to my surprise, she did. But two weeks after becoming a full-time mom, she was crying again.

"I can't be home all day and night." She had worked all her life, and she missed being a nurse. She went back to work part-time and remained a part-time nurse until both our children were in school.

That took some of the pressure off, but nevertheless, making money in the insurance business was no longer optional. I discovered that my anemic list of contacts was actually a boon. Nine out of ten hired agents in the insurance industry don't stay. They get to the end of their "Whom Do You Know?" books, and they find it too difficult to sell to strangers. But from the beginning, I enjoyed meeting and talking with new people.

My method was simple: "Treat every client as if they are going to be your client for life." Each prospective client got my best advice, whether this meant I'd make any money or not. Often, I'd spend a couple hours with someone and walk away with no money because they didn't need any of the policies New York Life had to offer. I began to build relationships, get referrals, and soon enough, earn a living.

I accepted any call that came into the front desk at New York Life. Unsolicited calls were usually about small insurance policies, and so the experienced agents didn't want to take them—they wouldn't provide enough return for their time. But for me, any return was a plus, and so one afternoon I found myself sitting at a dining room table with a woman who wanted advice about health insurance policies to supplement her Medicare. She already had her policies in hand and only wanted me to look them over and advise her. The policies she had were fine, and New York Life couldn't offer her a better deal. I left without thinking anything of it.

Until a few weeks later. Our receptionist put a call through to me from Channel 9 News in Washington, DC.

"Mr. McCormick," the production assistant on the line said, "we'd like to send a camera crew out with you to film you talking with one of your clients."

I had to wonder if the guy was crazy—he certainly couldn't be that hard up for news in DC. "Why on earth would you want to do that?"

"Oh, you don't know? Your name is in a congressional report on ethical insurance practices."

I still didn't know what he was talking about, but thanked

him and told him there was no reason to put my clients in what might be an uncomfortable situation—but would he please send me a copy of the report? Sure enough, when it arrived, there was my name. Apparently, Congress was working on new insurance regulations and the meeting about Medicare supplements had been a set-up they'd organized for research. Of fifty agents put in the same situation, eight had responded in a way the congressional committee deemed "highly ethical." My name was among the eight.

* * *

My office door at New York Life was always open—it was my way of recreating the community feeling I'd once had on front porches and around cafeteria tables. As other agents passed in the hall, they would often stop in to talk one-on-one about life and work.

I started to ask them the same question that I'd asked time and again at New York Telephone.

"What do you think about this job?"

And, to my chagrin, the responses were similar: "It's okay for now, but in the long run, the benefits are pretty good."

By this time, Confucius's advice—"Find a job you love, and you'll never have to work another day in your life"—had already replaced some of my thoughts about work. I couldn't reconcile this with what the other agents were telling me.

The contracts at New York Life were "back-end loaded," which is to say that the longer agents stayed, the larger their commission. And because agents received a percentage each time a client renewed a policy, commissions could add up as client bases grew. Twenty years was the cutoff—after twenty years, agents could expect to start receiving a nice income based on their total sales. If I left before twenty years, New York Life would win and I would lose. This policy was so well designed that agents at other companies called it "New York Life's golden handcuffs."

Most of us don't take well to handcuffs of any kind, and neither do I. I was already feeling constrained by only being permitted to sell New York Life policies. Often, the best possible policies for my clients weren't available for me to recommend because the best wasn't a New York Life policy. It was time for me to move on again.

Serendipitously, my manager asked me just at that time if I had any interest in going into management. Since I had been doing fairly well by New York Life standards, he had begun inviting me to speak to groups of new agents, and he'd taken a liking to my mantra of, "Treat each client as if they're going to be your client for life." I was looking for a change of direction, and after talking it over with my wife, I accepted his offer.

My new boss took me out to lunch. When we got to the restaurant, he set a thick three-ring binder down on the table. I glanced at the cover: *Management Policies*. As we waited to order, he opened it to the first page and started running down a checklist of all my new responsibilities as assistant manager.

By the time he got to the third page—and there were at least fifty more to go—I had had enough. After four years at New York Life, I had an insurance practice that, coupled with my wife's part-time income, meant we could support our family. Even as we had our second child, I was able to keep a little thinking and reading time for myself. And now, as my manager turned the pages of his binder, it seemed to me that each item he ticked off his list read simply, "You will have to jump through these hoops."

I reached across the table, closed the binder, and said, "I'm sorry, but I'm not the man for this job." And as quickly as it had begun, my career with New York Life ended.

* * *

I became an independent insurance broker. New York Life got to keep my renewal income, and I had to start from scratch, but in my mind I had solved the eternal riddle. Not only was I now able to do the best for my clients by offering them any company's policies, I was also my own boss. And my time was truly my own.

I now had the time and the inclination to be an active member of my neighborhood and the surrounding community. Not long after we got married, and while my career at New York Life was just beginning, my wife and I bought a fixer-upper home in need of some serious repairs on a beautiful lot in Vienna, Virginia. The house had a giant black walnut tree in its backyard. It was so big that it shaded the entire house. When my children were born, I hung a swing for them from a limb twenty feet off the ground. It swung in a beautiful, exhilarating arc. Over time, I think I pushed every kid in the neighborhood on that swing. And though my family has moved on, and our home has been torn down, the swing remains, hanging from that black walnut tree.

I worked on our house using the skills my father taught me. With the help of friends and neighbors, I put two additions on it, and with the help of my wife, we turned it into a place our children could grow up in. We had decided the moment we first set foot in the house with our bags and boxes that this would be the family home. Our children would not have to go through the dislocation I experienced when we left South Buffalo for North Buffalo.

And we both would know all our neighbors. We wanted to live in a neighborhood where everyone felt connected. And so the first summer we lived there, we asked our new neighbors if they'd be interested in throwing a block party for the Fourth of July. We closed down the street and everyone—families from twenty homes—brought tables and lawn chairs and set out potato salad and sandwiches. Everyone in the neighborhood was invited, and everyone showed up.

It happened to be a piercing hot, cloudless Fourth of July, and before too long, someone said, "Why don't we move the party to your backyard, where it's shaded?" And that's where it was every year after that, for thirty years. Our next-door neighbors were once professional singers, and so at every party their musician friends would come and play the saxophone, the trumpet, or even just grab a harmonica. Live music became the staple of our parties.

Pretty soon, we added a Halloween party to the program, where every year we'd decorate, and I'd cook a big pot of vegetarian chili and start an "illegal" bonfire in the backyard. And then we started celebrating New Year's Eve together, with all the kids at the next-door neighbors' house and all the adults at our house—and we'd all convene in our family room for the countdown.

I may not have been entirely free from the influences of growing up in Buffalo in the 1950s, but I was determined not to impose the same constraints on my children. As a boy in Buffalo, I hardly ever saw a black person. They did not live in my neighborhood, and they did not go to my school. I can still remember the day a black man walked down our street in South Buffalo. Immediately, neighbors were on the phone with each other saying, "What's he doing? What's going on? Should we call the police?"

Our neighborhood in Vienna could not have been more different. Only twelve miles west of DC, it is the home of people who come from all over the world to work and study in the embassies, non-governmental organizations, and language and

Don't Drink the Water

cultural centers that our capital is brimming with. Our neighborhood was truly mixed—not only a home to both black and white Americans, but also immigrants and visitors from India, Pakistan, China, and Korea. I put up a basketball hoop in our driveway, and some days I'd come home to find fifteen kids playing basketball. Ben and Greta might be the only Caucasians in the group.

Without my being aware of it, other people started to notice my commitment to the community. One day, someone asked me if I was willing to be president of the neighborhood civic association. That seemed great to me—it was a way of widening the circle of connectedness. I was president for five years, and I had a hand in some interesting projects. I noticed that the center courtyard of my kids' school was overgrown with weeds and seemed like a squandering of potential for a beautiful gathering space. So, with volunteers from the neighborhood, we planted gardens with flowers and dogwood trees. With the help of a good friend, I built four picnic tables where the kids could sit and have lunch. It became a living space, and when the next group of parents arrived, they took on the maintenance. It's still there, still beautiful, and the picnic tables are still in use.

People liked those picnic tables. Over the course of two or three years, I built five or six for neighbors who had a place for them. When I finished one, I'd go over to the neighbor's house and say, "Hey, would you help me haul something?" Together, we'd carry the table to their yard. It was my way of saying "Thank you" for the sense of connectedness we had with one another. On the Fourth of July, we'd drive around the block in a pickup truck, gathering up the tables and hauling them to my backyard so everyone could sit and eat.

I wasn't too aware that my many projects were starting to

add up until one day a friend of mine burst into my office holding the *Vienna Times*.

"Have you heard?" she said, a big smile on her face. She held up the newspaper and there was a photo of me on the front cover. "You're the *Vienna Times* Citizen of the Year!"

* * *

I was learning what it meant to be an active, contributing member of a community. And at the same time, I wanted to continue learning about the world at large. Years before, when I worked at New York Life and commuted into DC, I got in the habit of keeping a beach chair in the backseat of my car. Every morning I'd have to take a bridge over the Potomac River to get to work. After the bridge, the road branched, and I had a choice. If I turned right, I'd continue on to my office, but if I turned left, I could go to a beautiful park on the northern bank of the Potomac, where I could set up my chair and read. More often than not, I went left.

I kept—and still do keep—that chair in my car, and even after I moved my office to Vienna so that I could work in the community where I lived, I continued to find spots to read and think. If I had chosen to spend as much time in organized academic programs as I spent in that chair throughout my life, I might have a string of degrees after my name. But I did not want to follow a prescribed path, on which the knowledge I gathered would be directed or limited. Today I am not an expert in any field, but I have picked up a working knowledge in the areas that tapped my curiosity. I realize now that those mornings in the park were the beginning of a lifetime of research. I was looking for answers.

My curiosity touched on everything. My path did not follow any chronological order; rather, I let one question lead me to the next, and so I made my way from Socrates, Plato, and Aristotle to Thomas Aquinas, Thomas Merton, and Marilyn Ferguson. Sometimes I returned to the thinkers I'd read at Canisius—to Hegel and Nietzsche—but I went beyond Western thought as well, reading the works of Siddhartha Gautama, Lao Tzu, Confucius, the dalai lamas, Mahatma Gandhi, and others.

My questions led me from the large-scale to the minuscule. I landed on astrophysics for a while. I reread with new curiosity the story that I had learned as a child of Galileo confirming with his telescope what Copernicus had only been able to suggest with calculations—that the earth is not the center of the universe. The Western world's conception of itself depended so much on the earth's being the center that no one was willing to perform the thought replacement. Galileo handed his contemporaries the tool to observe the truth with their own eyes, but in the end he had to recant to save his life. I was struck anew by this timeless proof that thoughts, even false ones, can be so ingrained that killing each other to uphold them becomes a reasonable course of action for reasonable people.

Galileo's story was to me a metaphorical illustration of the smallness the aggregate can impose on each one of us. But I also began to see our smallness in measurable, physical terms. I studied the size of the universe, and how our concept of its vastness is ever expanding with our evolving knowledge and technology. Today, our technology allows us to see objects thirteen billion light years away: in other words, when light emanates from one of these distant objects, it takes thirteen billion years to reach us. This was a mind-boggling realization. When we truly allow ourselves to digest this fact, the emphasis we place on ourselves and our role in the universe has to shift. We are so very small. But so very connected—like the distant stars, we are part of the universe.

I was fascinated, too, to find out that every star has a shelf life—that it will eventually explode. That shelf life happens to be billions of years, but when the star finally explodes, the debris shoots outward and there's nothing in space to stop it—no friction, no wind. It travels and travels until it gets sucked into the gravitational field of another star, and there it congeals into a planet. That's how planetary systems develop. At the start, everything—and *everyone*—is star stuff.

Once I knew about the immense, I wanted to understand the very, very small. I turned to microphysics. I discovered David Bohm, a quantum physicist with the ability to write in layman's terms. At the end of one of his books, he mentions J. Krishnamurti, a philosopher whom he describes as the clearest thinker he has ever come across. That was exactly what I was looking for: clear thinking. After reading the transcripts of Krishnamurti's talks, I had to agree with David Bohm. I had found my tower crane in the world of philosophy.

When Krishnamurti was only a boy growing up in India, he was "discovered" by a worldwide spiritual organization, and it was decided then that he would be the organization's next great teacher. They saw something in this young, timid boy, and they decided he was what they were looking for. They groomed him for his leadership role, and he studied, under their guidance, every major religion and spiritual movement in the world. For years, he worked intensely, applying his young mind to the limits of human thinking, to ideas that most of us may not encounter in a lifetime.

On his twenty-first birthday, he was to make his first speech as the new leader. He stood up and announced that he was dissolving the organization. He said, "There are no gurus."

Krishnamurti had come to understand over the course of his studies that anyone who says, "Follow me, I know the path," couldn't possibly know where they are going—and he would not make the same error. The continual search for someone to follow, Krishnamurti told the assembled members of the organization, is pointless. We are all on the same path.

I went to see Krishnamurti speak at his last public appearance outside of India, which happened to be at the Kennedy Center in Washington, DC. He was ninety years old. My friends complained at the end of the speech that the sound system was terrible and they couldn't understand what Krishnamurti was saying. I can't explain how, but even with my hearing loss caused by years of construction work, I wasn't even aware of the sound problem. I heard every word.

* * *

I was happy. I had a young family, a wonderful community, and I was successful in my career. I was an independent businessman maintaining an office and a home in a town I held dear. I could step outside my house and say hello to the people who passed by. I could walk two blocks from either my house or my office to pick up my children from school. I had time to explore the questions that arose in my mind about my world. In every respect, I had everything I needed—not just food, clothing, and shelter, but love and fulfillment.

And yet, when I picked up the newspaper waiting at the end of our driveway every morning, I saw the same headlines across the front page that had gripped my heart as a boy. I had made the decision to return to the cage; I had shaped it to fit me, and I was contributing back to it. Everything I'd ever been told had led me to believe that I was doing what I could to make the world a better place. And still, when I picked up the paper, I saw these headlines. And every three or four months, I found a quiet place, and I cried.

Chapter Nine

However intense may be a group's moral conviction of the rightness of its particular religion or ideology, it should in its own interest function within the universally accepted system of law and politics aimed at order and justice.
—Quincy Wright, Professor of International Law,
University of Chicago

I started going into the woods. Twice a year, for a week in the spring and a week in the fall, I went on camping trips, alone in the Roanoke Valley in the spring or the Adirondack Mountains in the fall. I found isolated spots only accessible by water, primitive in every sense of the word. I called these trips my sabbaticals.

At first, these camping trips had nothing to do with solitude. They were about parenting. Every spring break, I would take my two children and two of their friends each—six children in all—camping. We went away from the city, away from newspapers and television and phone calls and noise, and we spent a week playing.

I still joke with my children, now adults, that I became a father so that I could have playmates. The older we get, the harder it is to find people willing to play. With each passing year, more and more of us seem to forget the importance of play as we blend into the steady seriousness of working life. It was as if I suddenly woke up one day a grown-up, and looking around me, I couldn't understand where all the players had gone.

But kids? They're always game. Hide and seek, flashlight tag, Red Rover, or games invented out of free time and open space

. . . you name it, they're in. And out in the woods, I was able to simply *be* with my children. It was parenting distilled, the same as it was two thousand years ago and the same as it will be two thousand years from now. It was my best shot at realizing Mr. Steinhelper's long-ago lesson—instead of teaching my children how to do human things, I hoped to teach them things about being human.

Over time, as my children got older and became more involved in school activities and navigating the ever-more-complex world of adolescence, they were less eager to go on camping trips with Dad. And so I went alone. I still played, though. I'd bring three softballs to juggle, or I'd invent games for myself with trees as goalposts and the downward slope of a hill as my opponent.

And I'd think. The trips gave me the time and space to pursue thoughts to their conclusion. I was dropping out of day-to-day existence—out of my habitual pattern of thinking in spurts punctuated by work and obligations. Or perhaps more accurately, I was dropping *in*—into an existence more aware and more connected. I was dropping into my search for answers. The kind of answers a man who cries for no apparent reason is desperate for.

* * *

My search for answers continued in my real world—the world of Vienna, Virginia—as well. It brought me, ultimately, to a seat on the town council.

It had become my habit to attend Vienna town council meetings as part of my role as the president of my neighborhood's civic association. At one of these meetings, a local activist from the nearby town of Falls Church stood up. He told us the story of how he had helped organize the effort to build a bridge on the Washington & Old Dominion Trail, a 45-mile-long bike trail that runs from DC to Purcellville, Virginia, which two million people use a year. In Falls Church, the trail crosses Route 7—a major commuter thoroughfare. The intersection was dangerous for bikers and pedestrians, and so this local activist had successfully-petitioned the town of Falls Church to install a bridge across Route 7. Now, bikers are able to cross the street without risk, and the town enjoys a beautiful piece of architecture in a place where thousands of people pass by foot, bicycle, and car every day.

The same bike trail runs through Vienna. Just as with Route 7 in Falls Church, it intersects with Maple Avenue in Vienna, the busiest artery in the town and the dividing line between north and south Vienna. The bike trail meets Maple Avenue in the middle of a block, and so, at the time, bikers were forced to either walk several yards down to the crosswalk, or risk darting across the middle of a four-lane highway.

"Why not build a bridge?" the activist asked us.

I listened to his ideas, and when he was done, I heard the town council's response. Bafflingly, at least to me, they didn't seem interested in the proposal. Because this man was a resident of Falls Church and not Vienna, there wasn't much for him to do beyond presenting his idea, and it seemed likely to me by the end of the meeting that it would die on the table. So I caught up with the man in the hallway as he was leaving and thanked him for his interest in our town.

"Listen," I told him, "this is a good idea. I'll see what I can do from here."

In Vienna, when a proposal has merit and the town council wants the citizens' input, they call a public hearing. That's all I wanted for the bridge idea. I wanted to hear what other citizens thought about it and to have an intelligent, open discussion rather than sitting back and waiting for the council to make a closed-door decision. But the town council had already decided, without citizen input, to move forward on installing a traffic light at the bike trail intersection. With the help of many other citizens—and eventually, with the backing of thousands of them—we worked for months on getting a public hearing called to discuss the benefits of a bridge versus a traffic light. But the town council never agreed to it. To this day, I cannot understand why.

I started by asking a council member what I needed to do to have a public hearing called. He said, "Bring us a petition with two hundred signatures."

So I stood at the intersection of Maple Avenue and the bike trail and collected signatures. In a very short time, I returned to the council with two hundred signatures. They told me that wasn't enough. I went back to the intersection and collected more. Still, that wasn't enough. Incrementally, the petition grew to three thousand signatures . . . and, still, the town council did not call a public hearing. The bridge had the support of the local business community and thousands of residents. But the council members had dug in their heels.

I went back to the same council member. "What else can I do?" I asked him. "What more do you need from us?" By this time, I had put together the Citizens for a Bridge committee, and we had over thirty residents as members.

His answer was, "Maybe you should think about taking a communication class, so you'll know how to talk to the council."

I walked away dumbfounded. I needed to enroll in a class to learn to talk to my elected representatives? In my mind, they should be learning how to listen to citizens!

I put the word out that at the next open meeting of the town council, I would represent our committee and request the public

Don't Drink the Water

hearing on the matter of the bridge. When the meeting came, the chamber was filled with Vienna residents and business owners who had come to support the idea.

As I was making the case for the bridge, I looked up at the mayor, who was seated in the center of the half-round, flanked by council members. I could tell by the repetitive motion of the pen in his hand that he was doodling.

"Mr. Mayor," I said. "Am I boring you?"

He was startled. "I'm just taking notes."

I knew then that our bid was over. The town council had never intended to grant a public hearing on the issue.

Although in some circles, I'm still called "the bridge guy," not getting the public hearing was not what bothered me. It was the way I was treated. The council members were all respected citizens, but I thought there should be at least one member of the council who returned the same level of respect that he enjoyed to every citizen with a new idea. I decided to run for my first and only political office—and I was elected.

Somehow, I thought the transition from citizen activist to town council member would be easy. I was wrong. I was now sitting at the table with the same people who had thought my bridge activities had overstepped the clearly defined Vienna boundaries of citizen activism. Their reaction to one of my first projects as a council member—locating and labeling the oldest tree in Vienna—set the tone.

On a trip home to Buffalo, I had seen a plaque on a giant sycamore tree on Franklin Street identifying it as the oldest tree in the city, and I thought, "That's a good idea. Vienna ought to have one, too." With over a hundred submissions from town residents, we found the oldest tree in Vienna. The black walnut in our yard was one of the top ten, but not the oldest. That title went to a giant white oak. We didn't do any harm to the tree; the plaque marking it as Vienna's oldest tree is set in a stone in the middle of a small garden at its base.

A local news station called me up for an interview after hearing that I had organized the contest. I told them, "I think the town arborist would have more interesting things to say than I do." Unfortunately, he was a bit of a recluse. He declined to be interviewed, and with no one better for the spot, the news team came back to me.

At our next closed-door council meeting, one of the other members was withdrawn and tense. He shifted in his seat and sighed whenever I spoke.

I couldn't let the session close without resolving the issue. I finally asked him, "Is something bothering you?"

He grabbed a piece of paper off the table before him and held it up. "What the fuck is this?" he said.

I looked closer. It was a memo announcing my upcoming interview with the local news.

"You're going to be on TV talking about that damn tree."

"I wasn't looking for an interview—" I started.

"Bullshit."

For a moment, the room was silent.

"So I'm a liar, too?" I asked.

He didn't answer.

I looked at the other members seated around me. "Is this how you all feel?"

No one spoke up.

The status quo on the council had always been that when a council member spearheaded a project, he was almost invariably doing it for personal political gain. If he was successful, the other council members figured they were guaranteed to see that project come up in his next campaign. It was impossible for me to convince my new colleagues that I wasn't worried about the next election—I honestly just wanted to work on projects. During my five years on the council, I found myself continually butting up against this obstacle.

Over time, however, I slowly gained some respect from my fellow council members. They were genuinely interested in doing their best for the town—they were just used to their own way of getting there. Eventually, I was able to show them that, unorthodox approach or not, my concern, like theirs, was for our community. The same mayor whom I had once challenged for doodling during my speech became a friend, and there were many visits to the Vienna Inn for beers after our council meetings.

About two years into my tenure on the council, I confronted a challenge that reaffirmed for me the role individual citizens can play in influencing decisions that affect them. I'd often run into the assumption that we as individuals have less and less ability to play a part as the level of organization of human activity gets increasingly complex. At home in our own families—of course, we get to make the decisions. In our neighborhoods? Sure, we can have a say. In our communities? Well, we can probably be heard—depending on the size of the community. Beyond that, we start to get nervous. We think it's out of our hands. But the opposite is true—the greater the level of organizational complexity, the more *it is up to us*.

The metro station in Vienna is the last station on the western end of the system's orange line. And critical to any final stop in any metro system is parking. Suburban commuters drive to the station, park, and take the train to and from work. Only a short time after the Vienna station opened, it became evident that more parking places were needed.

There happened to be a seven-acre parcel sitting empty next to the station. I had often wondered, while circling the Vienna metro station parking garage futilely looking for a space, why that parcel of land wasn't used for additional parking. As a council member, I finally discovered why. The parcel had been purchased ten years earlier by a major Virginia development company run by a man named Til Hazel. He had already secured the necessary permission to build a 600,000-square-foot office development on the land, but he had halted the project due to unfavorable economic conditions.

And now, ten years later, Mr. Hazel was resuming his plans—with one revision. Rather than building 600,000 square feet, he now wanted to build 1,100,000 square feet on the site.

I would later learn that he had contributed a tremendous amount of resources, time, and thought to Virginia education. He was interested in the long-term health of the state, and he had used his wealth and power to that end countless times. He was a decent man. But he was backing a bad idea.

When this proposal was put forth, I was sitting on one of the county's committees for reviewing development requests, as a representative of the town of Vienna. My role was to offer the town's perspective, and it was clear to me that adding a 1,100,000-square-foot office and hotel complex right next to an end station already cramped for parking space would be a mistake. As if the added parking logjam weren't bad enough, one of the main routes to the metro goes directly through Vienna. The increase in traffic created by the new complex would only exacerbate what was already a problem—commuter traffic on residential streets.

Naively, perhaps, I thought we had a fairly open-and-shut case for rejecting the proposal. I presented the facts to the town council.

When I was finished, the longest-tenured council member turned to me and said, "Don't tilt at windmills, Bob. Til Hazel is one of the most powerful men in Virginia. This is a done deal. Give it up."

I wasn't prepared to give up anything. The development was a bad idea; its backing by a powerful special interest didn't change that. I made my case at the next Fairfax County development meeting. I started an ad hoc citizens group, and we had buttons made. "No more!" was our slogan. All parties had agreed on 600,000 square feet—no more.

Still, it seemed that the plans would go forward. Not knowing what else to do, I made an appointment to meet with Til Hazel at his office.

I think Mr. Hazel works in the only office complex with its own exit off the DC beltway. His office, of course, is on the top floor. When I walked in the door, there he was, sitting behind his desk with the same flattop haircut my dad used to wear. The bulldog look. And, just as my father might have been, he was gruff and to-the-point.

"Mr. McCormick," he said, "we've done our projections. With the economy as it is now, it's just not worth it to build less than a million square feet on that parcel. We've already spent hundreds of thousands of dollars on plans. We must move forward."

I opened my briefcase, took out a letter, and slid it across the desk to him. It was a copy of the agreement for only 600,000 square feet that he had made ten years before with Fairfax County and with the town of Vienna. At the bottom of the page was his signature.

I pointed to it. "Is that your signature, Mr. Hazel?"

When he saw his own signature on the page, it made for an awkward moment. But times had changed, and a ten-year-old signature had apparently passed his statute of limitations. He wasn't willing to back down. We ended our meeting cordially, both agreeing to disagree, but I think he realized that I did not plan on backing down either. And I, not having any other recourse, returned to gathering signatures on our petition against the development.

By the time the proposal went to a vote with the Fairfax County Supervisors, we had gathered over five thousand signatures and had presented a strong case. The county supervisors decided that the proposal for 1,100,000 square feet was a bad idea. They would grant no more than 600,000 square feet. And in the end, Til Hazel and his partners decided to build residential units on the site. A residential development brings in about one-tenth the volume of traffic that an office building of comparable size does. We were aiming to keep the adverse consequences minimal, never dreaming that in the end, we'd eliminate them altogether.

From that experience, and many more like it on the town council, I began to understand that although the chances of losing a fight may appear great, that is no reason not to fight. A good idea, like the bridge for the bike trail, will always have a fighting chance no matter how humble its backing. A bad idea, like the metro station development, can be defeated no matter how strong its backing . . . as long as enough of us agree that it must be.

We will always live with powerful special interests; there are simply too many human beings, and we are too social, to pretend otherwise. We cannot live isolated in a hovel here and a hovel there. So, unless we all decide that we never want to change or evolve, ever, we cannot use the mere existence of powerful special interests to keep us from moving forward. Not every obstacle is a windmill.

Chapter Ten

Never have the nations of the world had so much to lose or so much to gain. Together we shall save our planet or together we shall perish in its flames. Save it we can and save it we must, and then shall we earn the eternal thanks of mankind and, as peacemakers, the eternal blessing of God.
—John F. Kennedy

On the morning of September 12, 2001, I went to my wife and told her I planned to resign from the town council.

The previous evening, still under the cresting wave of that day's shock and grief, my wife and I had invited all our neighbors to come over and sit on our porch. Dozens of us gathered there, of all ages. I didn't have anything I planned to say—none of us did. It just seemed important to sit in each other's company and to do what we could to comfort each other.

It was a healing evening for all of us, but I was to discover that no amount of community ethos could temper the struggle we each had yet to face, individually, to come to terms with the events of September 11. My reaction was not unique—my life was changed, as so many lives were. Some lost a loved one, some went to war, and some continue to live in the center of that war and all its consequences. I do not wish to suggest that, especially when compared to those so immediately affected by the attacks, there was anything remarkable or exceptionally profound in my experience, and so it doesn't seem necessary to describe it. Suffice it to say that I understood, irrevocably, that I could not continue to meet the world as I had been.

My tears were a small clue, and now I had irrefutable proof: my attempts to create peace and satisfaction for myself and my family by thinking about the world and my place in it on a local, small scale were no longer enough. I simply could not imagine going back to my daily activities as they had always been. To be a member of the town council meant spending a tremendous amount of time thinking about what was best for our Vienna community. But now my priorities for my thought time had shifted. I needed to feel a part of a different community, a community that included all of us: the global community. It's unfortunately parochial, but though I had been confronted with headlines describing events as unthinkable as those of September 11 all my life, it wasn't until I found myself at the scene of the crime that I was permanently moved to action beyond tears.

My wife convinced me to serve out my term on the council. "The citizens elected you, and you owe them that much," she said. And she was right.

So, for another ten months, I was a council member for Vienna. But I was not a good one. I was preoccupied. At one point near the end of my term, a representative of the Democratic Party approached me, although I was and am an independent, to say that the party had taken note of my activities and high vote tallies in Vienna. Would I be interested in running for state office? I told him no—I was leaving politics. When everything changes in the span of a day, we have to do what we can to answer the question, "What now?" And my method, as it has always been, was to do research and think.

In my mind, this wasn't an American or European or Asian or African or Middle Eastern problem; it was a human problem. Somehow, perhaps only in recent decades or perhaps over the whole course of human history, we had learned to accommodate a world where the logic of terrorism was possible. Terrorism had become, for a growing number, a justifiable response to human activity—not simply in the United States, but all over the world.

I came across the story of a Palestinian man who had five sons. Four of the five had already died as suicide bombers, and this father's one hope and prayer was that his fifth son would follow them. Perhaps you label that man's feeling "hatred." Perhaps you call it "anger" or "pride." Whatever its name, it was so strong that he would gladly give up all five of his sons for the cause.

It's a story that is easily jarring to an American reader. But it is possible to find US citizens who share that man's level of commitment to a cause. When I read his story, I thought about how we Americans feel toward the men and women who give their lives for the American cause—whether we call it "freedom," "democracy," or "all we hold dear." That feeling is part of the human condition. When a human being kills someone for personal gain, we call him a *murderer*. When he kills for national gain or religious belief, we call him a *hero* or a *martyr*. In the end, to the parents of a child caught in the crossfire, he is the same.

It didn't seem possible to me, then, that the September 11 attackers had acted because they "hated our freedoms." I wasn't buying that explanation. It would be a very difficult argument to make to convince a man first to hate the cultural freedoms of a people in a faraway place, and then to give his life for that hatred. I couldn't imagine anyone making that argument to a group of young recruits and being successful. But if hatred of our freedoms wasn't the explanation, there had to be another one. Something was wrong. What was it?

I started by studying global weaponry. I learned that with our tax dollars, United States citizens supply over 50 percent of the world's exports of weaponry—and this in the pursuit of greater national security. We make up only 4 percent of the world's population, yet we spend more on weaponry than the rest of the world combined. While we are spending over $600 billion on our military each year, the United Nations estimates that it would cost only $62 billion annually to eliminate poverty, hunger, and illiteracy throughout the world. No cooperative effort between countries has been launched to make good on the potential implied by that UN study. Instead, thirty thousand children die every day from diseases with known cures. I snagged on that fact for days—perhaps for the rest of my life. Thirty thousand children . . . that's every last kid in the city of Buffalo dying every day.

These were, perhaps, facts that I should have been aware of. But I was wrapped up—as so many of us are, as it is so easy to be—in the immediate, in the small-scale all around me. I had turned over the responsibility for reacting to these facts to others. And since childhood, reaccepting this responsibility had been tugging at my coattails. From those newspapers I flung as a boy to the computer and television screens that now surround me, I—and all of us—live in a world where global communications have made us all eyewitnesses. We have the tools to witness the totality of human suffering—war, poverty, disease, starvation.

When a crime between individuals is committed out of sight, there is one victim and one perpetrator. But when that crime is committed before an eyewitness, there are two victims. The eyewitness must bear the psychological ramifications of her experience, and she must bear her human responsibility, whether fulfilled or unfulfilled, to the victim. She might, out of the universal impulse of empathy, attempt to intervene on the victim's behalf. But she might also, out of the equally universal and equally valid impulse of self-preservation, remain on the fringe. Say she does.

Say there's nothing she can do. What will she do the second, third, or fourth time she witnesses the same crime? She will learn to accommodate it. She will learn to shoulder her helplessness and trudge forward, eyes averted.

This is the same accommodation television and the Internet have taught us. We witness from afar, and we trudge forward. But though we compartmentalize, though we find ways to continue on with our immediate, personal-scale lives, the psychological ramifications of being eyewitnesses are with each of us at every moment. To shoulder that helplessness, we turn increasingly away from it and into ourselves, just to get through.

Now, for the first time, I was realizing that there was an alternative to turning away and finding quiet places to cry: I would share what I had found out with as many people as I could.

I gathered together the facts I was learning and created a presentation. I focused on US weaponry—how much of it there is, how much it costs, and where in the world it all ends up—and I gave talks about it at meetings of local groups, like the Optimist Club and the Lions Club. I quickly learned that I had to refine my approach. Some people, many whom I had considered friends, stopped talking to me after they heard me speak. They thought that I was being un-American, but in my mind the talks were the exact opposite. I was interested in discussing the ideals upon which this country was founded. We are all equal, and we all have equal rights. At one point in human history, we were humanity's beacon of hope. It is not being un-American to want that title back. I didn't understand why our security and prosperity, and global security and prosperity, had to be mutually exclusive.

I created a new presentation with a broader perspective and hired some skilled and creative professionals to help me put it together technically. We invited activists in different fields from

Washington, DC and the surrounding area, and I gave the presentation at the Center for Innovative Technology near Dulles International Airport. Sixty-five people came.

We had created a slide show that I gave along with my talk. It was my best attempt at depicting clearly, graphically, the levels of human suffering that we aren't often exposed to. I wanted to show the audience realities that I was sure they were unaware of.

When I was finished, a woman in the audience raised her hand.

"We know all this," she said. "What do you propose we do about it?"

For several seconds, I stared blankly into the audience. I honestly hadn't considered the question. My insurance experience had taught me that people don't buy a policy unless they believe they need one. Likewise, before developing any solution to any problem, we have to know we need one. There I was, speaking to activists from across the spectrum, intelligent, involved, and creative people. It had seemed to me that all that was missing was a clear articulation of the need—and the solution would follow. But the need was already on the table and had been for a long time before I showed up. Somehow we had all come to accommodate that need because we couldn't see how to satisfy it.

I stopped talking for a while and went back to doing research. It wasn't long before I discovered that a way to satisfy the need was already on the table, too. And had been for decades, if not centuries.

* * *

Picture our world as a shining, blue-green ship at sea. Every last one of us, from the President of the United States of America to the youngest child in a rural Congolese village, is a passenger on that ship. Nothing separates us—and the vast, uninhabitable emptiness of the water contains us. We are alone at sea. There are no supply ships to bring us what we need and haul away what we don't. There are no rescue boats to call. There is no abandoning ship.

Our ship is not so big. We have the modern communications tools to see the beauty of every part of it and the beauty to be found in every culture on board. But we also see, with our own eyes, scenes of human violence, poverty, and ignorance that take place, whether below deck or in the open air. And, too, we have the modern weaponry to reach every corner of the ship. Nuclear bombs, the military choice of the rich, and terrorism, the military choice of the poor, threaten any sense of physical security for every single passenger, no matter what they are willing to pay for a secure berth.

Knowing that this is the ship we're on, how can we sail blithely forward? There is another generation waiting to board the vessel we are holding in trust for them. How can we expect them to feel secure on board while we continually stock the ship with new weaponry? How can we expect them to maintain their lifestyles after we've drained the ship's resources to maintain ours? How can we expect them to deal with the accumulating anger and hatred bred by the injustices of poverty, hunger, illiteracy, and deaths from preventable diseases—when we couldn't? How can we give them hope in one hand and a world without any workable, long-term vision in the other?

But what if we acted as mutual passengers on a shared journey toward the continual, long-term habitation of the planet Earth in a civilized manner? What if we developed the abstract thinking necessary to design our own future—to site the ship's course and steer it there together?

The solution I found and that I am now suggesting requires a global effort: first, to officially establish our common intergenerational long-term goals, and second, to create the plan or document or organization that will allow us to attain them. Only a group of globally empowered individuals, capable of adopting *a perspective that includes all of us* and all future generations, can accomplish this task.

What I am talking about is reorganizing humanity on the macro level. This does not mean eliminating national sovereignty in favor of a single world government, but it does require a level of global cooperation beyond that which our leaders engage in today.

As the author and futurist H. G. Wells wrote:

> *A federation of all humanity, together with a sufficient measure of social justice to ensure health, education, and a rough equality of opportunity, would mean such a release and increase of human energy as to open up a new phase in human history.*

That new phase can begin today—but we are going to have to ask for it.

This idea is not mine, nor is it new. After my presentation at the Center for Innovative Technology, I shifted my approach from defining the problem to asking the question, "What do we do about it?" And over time, I came across the answer—over and over again, in the words of past and present diplomats, politicians, scientists, and artists.

I saw it articulated by Winston Churchill, Golda Meir, Albert Einstein, Mahatma Gandhi, Pope John Paul II, and General Douglas MacArthur. It belongs to seven US presidents, from Ulysses S. Grant to John F. Kennedy Jr. to Ronald Reagan. It is even etched in stone on the Thomas Jefferson Memorial in Washington, DC, in his own words:

> *I am not an advocate for frequent change in laws and constitutions. But laws and institutions must go hand in hand with the progress of the human mind. As that becomes more developed, more enlightened, as new discoveries are made, new truths discovered and manners and opinions change, with the change of circumstances, institutions must advance also to keep pace with the times. We might as well require a man to wear still the coat which fitted him when a boy as civilized society to remain ever under the regimen of their barbarous ancestors.*

Knowing that I had stumbled on the solution and knowing, too, that I was not the first to do so, I started looking for organizations promoting global approaches to confronting our problems. I found them in the dozens—Greenpeace, Physicians for Social Responsibility, Union of Concerned Scientists, Oxfam, Earth Policy Institute, Search for Common Ground, Earthjustice, and the list goes on to include hundreds of non-governmental organizations designed to confront the problems caused by the way we currently conduct human activity. I learned that there are over forty professions that have formed "Without Borders" groups: Doctors Without Borders is the most well known, but there are also Engineers Without Borders, Teachers Without Borders, Clowns Without Borders . . . the NBA even runs a Basketball Without Borders program. But all of these organizations seemed to focus on treating the symptoms with the same institutions and organizations we were handed by previous generations, while ignoring our potential to cure the disease by creating new institutions and organizations instead.

The closest I came to finding a truly global perspective centered on our potential to create new institutions and organizations was the World Federalist Association. This was a group of people who at the time were interested, as I am, in reorganizing human activity on the macro level, in going beyond the first noble but failed attempts of the League of Nations and the United Nations to creating a workable system for global cooperation. But to me, the World Federalist Association was taking the wrong message to the wrong places.

First, their message offered people an untenable choice between two extremes. On the one hand, there was the status quo: an almost complete lack of global cooperation in favor of nationalism, a system that cannot effectively address the countless, interconnected issues that are not contained by national borders. On the other hand, however, the WFA presented "world government": a term that makes people balk at the possibility of a monolithic and controlling system overriding the world's cultural differences and threatening the human right to self-determination. Given the choice between a nonfunctional status quo and a potentially disastrous change, people will choose the status quo every time. The WFA was not talking about the thousands of options that lie between these two extremes—options that would allow us to enjoy the best of both worlds.

In addition, the WFA was taking their campaign for global change to United States congresspeople and senators. At their annual meeting, I offered that I thought their approach was wrongheaded. "Trying to influence those who are currently winning the game that's being played is a fool's errand," I said. "You should be taking your ideas to the ultimate decision-maker—the average American citizen."

I decided to do just that. With the help of friends and hired professionals, I founded the Global Plan Initiative. Our message was simple. We human beings are planners. We plan for our children's education, we plan for our retirements, we draw up plans for buildings, we plan offensives in war. But we don't have a workable long-term plan to guide human activity.

Just as I once asked that the idea of a bike trail bridge be given a fair, public discussion, I was now asking that the idea for a global plan be brought to the table. The idea is that *now is the time for our leaders to cooperate, as equals, on establishing a global cease-fire while we prepare for and hold a global summit where the topic is the long-term health of the entire human race.* And now is not the time to worry about the details.

I spoke on behalf of the Global Plan Initiative at every chance I got. And I discovered that everyone seemed to agree with the idea—we *do* need a long-term plan. But few people believed that we could get our leaders to agree on any plan—or even on a method for developing a plan. To many of the people I spoke with, I was whistling in the wind. But to me, I was learning to whistle.

In the beginning, I thought I had happened on such a good idea that it would simply be a matter of voicing it, and it would take off on its own. Soon enough, I wouldn't have to talk about it anymore. I'd place it in hands more capable than mine, and it would come to fruition. But months and eventually years later, I was still whistling. At first, my reaction was to increase the intensity. I tried to beat it into people's heads—and lost a lot of potential allies in the process.

When a radio signal doesn't match the frequency of the receiver, you don't solve the problem by turning up the volume. You change the frequency. It's not the listener's job to hear better;

it's the messenger's job to speak more clearly. Sensing my frustration, the others working on Global Plan Initiative gave me some advice: "Bob, you should write your thoughts down."

So I spent two years writing a collection of essays entitled *We Need a Plan*. When it was finally completed, a good friend of mine sent it out to over two hundred people, from past presidents to Nobel Peace Prize laureates to celebrated diplomats. Anyone she could come up with who was demonstrating their interest in global long-term thinking got a copy.

The response kept me going for a while, but it was minimal. We got a few positive answers, one from the philanthropist and education activist Bernard Rapoport. He called me up and said, "Who are you?"

"I'm Bob McCormick," I answered, half joking.

"No, I mean I've never heard of you. What are your credentials? Why are you interested in these questions?"

"I'm a US citizen," I said.

He told me that he thought *We Need a Plan* was the most remarkable thing he'd ever read.

I thought, "Finally. Someone is interested who will know what the next step is." I flew to Waco, Texas to meet him.

As I settled into my seat across from Mr. Rapoport's desk, he held up a thick, cream-colored piece of paper. "Do you know what this is?" he asked, a twinkle in his eye.

"What is it?"

"It's a personal invitation to Bill Clinton's sixtieth birthday party in New York!" He grinned, truly delighted to share the news.

The two of us sat in his office talking for most of the afternoon. But eventually, we came to the same impasse I'd reached before countless times . . .

"What can I do?" Mr. Rapoport wanted to know.

Don't Drink the Water

I didn't have an answer. I thought he would know what to do.

What he did offer was to write an endorsement for *We Need a Plan*, which he sent me not long afterward:

> *I came to my office a week or so ago and opened one of the 8.5 x 11 folders that usually has advertisements. Generally I throw this kind of mail away quickly. As I reached for the waste paper basket I saw the words, "We Need a Plan," so I decided to turn a few more pages. I am much richer today after having read this. Now I know: this is must reading for anyone wanting a better understanding of the seriousness of our problems and a recognition that there is indeed a workable answer. From my point of view, this is MUST READING.*

When I read this, I was thrilled. From all angles, I was being told that an average citizen couldn't make the arguments I was making. I needed higher credentials, stronger backing, an important title. Mr. Rapoport, it seemed to me, had edged me closer to credibility. But I also knew by then that no one owns an idea; it doesn't need credentials, and any one of us can present it.

He also put me in touch with the owner of a very successful PR firm. This man was also a personal friend of the Clintons, and at the time that I was in touch with him, he was already advising Hillary Clinton on her possible presidential primary campaign.

After he'd read *We Need a Plan*, he called me and asked, "Would you mind if a candidate for president co-opted the ideas in your pamphlet?"

Again, I was sure I had rounded the corner. "Of course not!" I told him. "They aren't my ideas to begin with."

He told me he would look me up the next time he came to DC. But I never heard from him again.

I never felt defeated, but I was becoming increasingly frustrated. I was sure that this idea was so good that all I needed to do was share it. And not knowing how to share it was causing a lot of sleepless nights for me and a lot of angst for my wife, who didn't know what to do with my relentless focus.

After a time, understandably enough, she didn't want to hear me talk about a global plan anymore. That was the beginning of the end. But I could not call off my pursuit. This was, in my mind, the only effort that mattered—all other efforts were secondary, and would ultimately fail if this one failed. And I was failing.

I left my home and my community and moved into a lonely, remote cabin in the woods, with only a lingering question to keep me company.

Had I failed where failure was unthinkable?

Chapter Eleven

*It is no measure of health to be well adjusted to
a profoundly sick society.*
—J. Krishnamurti

Thirty years before, I had closed the door of my old Chevy on the only life I'd ever known—and never felt so free.

Now, as I stood in the hallway of the Georgetown Hospital Mental Health Care Inpatient Unit—commonly referred to as the psych ward—I heard the double doors lock behind me, and instantly, I reencountered the weightlessness of being free.

Immediately to my right, there was a nurses' station. And to my left was a nondescript lounge, peppered with the kind of muted, stain-resistant furniture that graces hospital waiting rooms everywhere. A few people were perched here and there throughout the room, staring at magazines or through the curtains. They were all wearing cheerless, standard-issue variations on the psych ward theme: no drawstrings, no belts, no metal zippers. Nothing that could, with a little ingenuity and a lot of desperation, be repurposed for self-harm.

The dress code made it easy to identify who was there making a living and who was there wondering about living. I was, of course, part of the second set.

I didn't know what to expect from my new surroundings,

but I did know that, if anything, they were different from the place I'd just come from. And that was all I needed. To feel the doors shut between my past and my future.

I wasn't crying anymore. I had cried for two days, and then, just like that, I was done. As I stood there in the hallway, bewildered and infinitely relieved, I suddenly remembered a friend telling me that the composition of tears changes depending on the source of those tears. Tears of laughter are different from tears of pain. Tears of pain have a higher protein and hormone concentration; they literally wash out the body's toxins. Who knew if this was true or just a nice sentiment, but in that moment, it seemed reasonable to me.

An orderly showed me my room, which I would share with another patient. It was furnished with two narrow cots covered by thin foam mattresses. Like our clothing, the room was conspicuously safe. The lights were recessed overhead—no lamps with electrical cords. The windows were sealed and locked. And the door remained open to the hall.

The orderly told me I was welcome to sit in the lounge with the other patients, and then he disappeared. For the rest of my time there, my contact with him and his colleagues would barely go beyond "Good morning" and "Good night." I spent four days in the ward, and during that time, I can only remember seeing a doctor once. When I stepped into the room where she was to interview me, I found her sitting at a conference table surrounded by a dozen medical students. Her exam—a series of routine questions about why I thought I was there, followed by, almost as an afterthought, the results of my blood test—took ten minutes. The only piece of insight I gained was that, according to my blood test, I was woefully short on vitamin B12. The doctor told me that one of the most significant symptoms of B12 deficiency, which is common in vegetarians like myself, is depression.

I asked her, "How quickly can you get me B12?"

Two days later, they finally brought me the supplements—which are readily available over-the-counter. I had long since stopped crying. Clearly, my problem was not as simple as a vitamin deficiency.

I understood very quickly that the Mental Health Care Inpatient Unit was not a treatment facility. It was a holding tank. We sat around the lounge, and the nurses and interns kept an eye on us from their station across the hall. If we didn't manage to do ourselves harm, our stay was considered a success.

Once I understood these parameters, I began to think of my stay as a psychiatric coaching opportunity. I had arrived there entirely open to any suggestion—when you've cried for two days, you have to be. So, when I discovered that the Georgetown doctors would not be offering solutions or even talking to me, I decided to talk to my only other companions in the ward: my fellow patients.

There were only four of us staying there at the time, two men and two women. Often, we were joined by the husband of one of the women, who came every day to sit with her for hours—simply helping her, quietly, to wait it out. I would learn that four was an unusually low number for the ward, but for us, it was a welcome stroke of luck. We'd each been humbled by life's circumstances; we had nothing to protect and no images to sell. Talking became our pastime and our lifeline. Gathered around on the squeaking vinyl of the lounge chairs, we'd spend whole days sharing our worlds.

The other man in our group had been a cardiologist. Over the course of my stay there, each time we sat down together, more of his story would emerge. He had a private medical practice, he told us, and, due to some important advancements he had made in the field, he also held a prestigious teaching position at a nearby medical school.

"The practice has been . . ." he started to explain, then trailed off. "There have been some changes . . ." Again, he didn't finish.

The other patients and I didn't comment, but his story didn't add up. I'd come to understand that we had no reason to hide from each other, and every reason not to. Perhaps we couldn't solve each other's problems, but at least we could listen, sort through, *try*. We all sensed that the cardiologist was holding back; he was wrestling with something within himself. We didn't press him. We knew now from our own experience that the decision to speak without fear was a personal one.

It wasn't until the last day I was there that he finally finished his story.

"Listen, I haven't told you everything," he said. Of course, we'd known this all along.

"My wife did the books for my practice," he continued. "She was double-billing Medicare."

He had had no idea until his practice was suddenly closed down. When federal investigators came to him and asked that he testify against his wife, he couldn't bring himself to do it. He refused and was charged along with her. He served time in prison, but far worse, his license was revoked. He lost his practice, his teaching position, his house, and eventually the marriage he had sought to protect. His long fall had brought him inside the locked doors of the Georgetown psych ward.

Unlike the cardiologist, the two women patients confessed that they could not point to a single event in their lives as the explanation for their struggles. Both were educated professionals, and, like me, the best explanation they could offer was that they found it extremely difficult to cope with the world the way it is.

I talked with them about the Global Plan Initiative. This was one of the first times that I was able to share the idea without being met with immediate resistance, without hearing, "Give it up." We were just four people, stripped of our cultural labels, stripped of the daily need to grasp and strive, and looking only to understand how we had all come so perilously close to the edge. We were four willing, open minds. In a way, this was the first public hearing for the global plan, the hearing I'd been asking for all along. It was a small crowd, but it was a start.

One of the women gave a slight smile toward the end of one of our talks. "We're not crazy," she said, reaching for her ever-present husband's hand. "We're living in a crazy time."

Again and again in the ward, I thought of a favorite film of mine, *King of Hearts*. The film tells the story of a small French town at the end of World War I. German occupying forces are retreating from the town as the Allies advance, but they leave behind a bomb rigged to blow up a weapons cache and destroy the whole town with it. The French resistance catches wind of the plot, and long before the bomb explodes, the townspeople evacuate . . . with the exception of the residents of the local insane asylum.

Left to their own devices, the inmates of the asylum take over the town. They dress in the townspeople's abandoned clothes and lay claim to their abandoned roles. Some are priests, some are generals, some are prostitutes. When a lone Scottish soldier arrives to disarm the bomb, he can't understand why these French townspeople are so odd. Ultimately, their charm and joy win him over; he disarms the bomb, is crowned King of Hearts, and falls in love with a tight-rope-walking inmate named Poppy.

But then the winds change. The German battalion returns to the town to see why their bomb didn't explode—just as the

Scottish troops are marching in. The lunatics mistake the marching soldiers for a parade and watch delightedly from the town balconies . . . until the enemy troops spot each other and open fire. When all the soldiers on both sides lie dead in the square, the lunatics, one by one, begin to shed their costumes and finery and file solemnly back into the asylum. The film ends with the image of the Scotsman, the King of Hearts, standing at the asylum gate and waiting to be granted entry.

* * *

On a Friday, after four days in the ward, I was released. I exchanged contact information with my new friends, but we have not been in touch. Imagine if the inmates of *King of Hearts* had reunited outside the asylum after the French townspeople returned, repopulating the streets where the lunatics once held their dances and parades. Impossible. The ward was an experience that could not be replicated. But I will never forget my fellow patients or the four days we spent together—not *in*, but *out* of the cage.

My release was contingent on a doctor's recommendation that I enroll in an outpatient treatment program. For two weeks starting that Monday, I would spend eight hours a day, five days a week at the hospital. I knew I still needed help, and I gladly signed up.

But before I could start, I had to get through the weekend. Returning to that cabin in the woods was out of the question. So I booked a room at a hotel near the hospital and started walking around the neighborhood. The tears were behind me, but I was now alone, without the companionship of the three people who had understood me, however briefly. I knew that my confrontation with my demons had only just begun.

On Saturday, a good friend of mine spent the day with me walking around Georgetown, letting the noise and people distract us. We wandered in and out of shops, taking in the window displays and walking from one end of Georgetown to the other and back again. On Sunday, alone again, I made my way up the long hill to the National Cathedral.

For most of the afternoon, I sat on a bench below the main tower, staring up at the stones I had helped set decades before. The view was reversed, but in small spurts, I could remember the feeling. And I knew it hadn't changed. The world is not so big, and all of us share it.

I only spent one day in the outpatient program at Georgetown. At one point on Monday afternoon, I sat around a large table with a dozen other patients. A therapist gave us colored pencils and paper and asked us each to take a half hour to draw an important moment in our lives. At the end of the half hour, we went around the table, showing our drawings and explaining what they meant to us.

The first man to share showed a picture of a skull and crossbones. The woman beside him had drawn a prone figure with a black x over it. As we continued around the room, the other patients were all showing dark images, moments of hopelessness, stories of desperate struggle.

When it was my turn, I held up my paper. I had drawn the National Cathedral with a tower crane on top of it.

Shortly after, the doctors told me, "This is not the place for you." I had to agree.

They recommended regular visits to a particular holistic psychiatrist—a regimen of Mental Health Lite for a veteran of the psych ward. As with every other doctor I had come across since the cabin in the woods, I gave my new psychiatrist a copy of *We Need a Plan* and asked that he read it before we continued with treatment. I don't know if any of my other doctors had actually complied with that request except for one, a young resident who pulled me aside after he had read it and asked if there were any way he could help me with the cause. As always, I had told him I wasn't sure—that was just the problem.

My new psychiatrist cost $300 an hour. In our second meeting, I got my money's worth from him in a single sentence.

I had finished telling him about my failed attempts to communicate the idea for a global plan and how these had led me, ultimately, to the precipice.

He looked me in the eye and said simply, "You've got to get over the pain. *You've got work to do.*"

I knew instantly that he was right. In all my time at Georgetown, not a single doctor or patient I had spoken with had told me I should give up my work with the Global Plan Initiative. That wasn't the problem. But I could not continue through life crying and feeling bad about being human. The answer was to do the work I'd discovered was possible. And there was a lot of it ahead of me.

Slowly, over time, I began to unpack what that meant: "You've got work to do." I was, in the most literal way possible, out of the woods. On the same day that I returned to the National Cathedral, by sheer chance, I literally ran into a For Rent sign outside an English basement in the heart of Georgetown. So I rented it. And I moved forward with my new life and with the Global Plan Initiative, which I reimagined as Globalsummit.org.

The source of my pain was that I had lost the ability to accommodate the suffering I was witnessing. By this time, I knew with absolute certainty that human suffering is not an inevitable consequence of human activity. I had replaced that thought, and accommodation was no longer an option. I could not stop imagining a different world.

John Lennon used his talents as an artist to try to get us to *imagine*. Martin Luther King Jr. used his talents for oratory to try to get us to *dream*. We need these first steps. Without imagining and dreaming, there is nothing to create. But continually imagining and dreaming won't end anyone's suffering. Beyond imagining and dreaming, there's work to be done.

Right now, in our collective imaginations, we have no vision of ourselves being able to work things out. We are limited to our leaders' ideas about what we can accomplish, and these ideas are not based on a vision of the future, but on the worn road of the past. Our leaders are determined to address the global problems confronting our generation with the tools created by past generations. They just need more soldiers willing to die, more sophisticated weaponry, more resources, more funding, more studies, more treaties, more summits. They tell us that with all of the above and more time, we might eventually begin to effectively address the adverse consequences of current human activity—even as we proceed full speed ahead with the same activities that created those adverse consequences in the first place.

Our leaders are using human experience as the guide to set our goals. The time has come for us to go beyond our current leaders' imaginations and set new goals based on our potential, not on our experience.

We've got work to do.

Chapter Twelve

Our world is prodigiously healthy and vigorous, and terribly sick at the same time. The extraordinary upsurge and economic expansion of the past . . . give hope of unprecedented progress and welfare. The malady that may destroy everybody and everything is caused exclusively by our totally outdated political institutions—in flagrant contradiction to the economic and technological realities of our time.
—Emery Reves, *The Anatomy of Peace*

Far in the distance, surrounded on all sides by deep, velvet blackness, a tiny light is shining. At first he isn't sure he's seen it—it seems to pulse against its black background, so that it could be nothing more than a trick of his eyes after a long night of travel.

But even if his eyes might, the sensors on his dashboard don't lie. In the small, glowing screen near his right hand, a red light flashes. There are objects in the emptiness up ahead.

He taps a few buttons with one hand, exciting more sensors on the outside of his craft into alertness. With the other hand, he gently coaxes the throttle forward. His dash gives off a soft, low beep of warning, and then, in an instant, the craft accelerates.

He is traveling at a speed beyond speed. Outside the influence of any gravitational pull, in a realm where friction is unknown and impossible, his craft sails so quickly that its motion feels like stillness. His body is not thrust back against the pilot's seat; he does not have to brace against his safety restraints. He merely waits, relaxed, attentive, as his craft leaps across light years of space, and then slides to an unassuming halt at the center of a revolving constellation of light, color, wisps of gas, and bursts of energy.

These are the objects he saw from afar. One is an immense ball of explosions and heat, wrapped by the orbits of smaller, darker, but no less beautiful spheres. This is the place the screen in his dashboard labels System #622910472.

Immediately, one of the orbiting spheres catches his eye. While the others are dull browns or swirls of molten red, this one glows a cool, welcoming blue. At this distance, its surface seems alive with the soft caress of white gaseous clouds. Curious, he taps more keys on his dash, and his craft slides across the emptiness toward the blue marble before him.

Noiselessly, he continues his approach until the gravitational pull of the sphere is almost irresistible. Then he shifts the throttle and lets his craft slip into a wide orbit around the planet. At first, he is on a glowing side of the sphere, where its surface reflects back the tremendous light cast by this system's star. But as he travels along his orbit, he passes gradually to the other side of the sphere, where the planet's surface is in darkness, hidden from the radiating light of the star.

But still, the surface seems to glisten. He leans forward, peering down—and then he smiles. Lights. There is artificial light on the planet's surface. *It is inhabited by intelligent beings.*

Peering closer still, he sees that these lights are grouped in patterns. Some burn in large, vibrating clusters, others pepper the surface as solitary beacons. *These inhabitants are organized and social.*

He inputs a brief message to his base.

Hypothesis confirmed, he writes. *Planet #3 in System #622910472 sustains intelligent life. Descending to surface for further observation.*

With a low beep, the screen confirms that his message has been transmitted successfully. He does not hesitate or wait for a response. He plugs coordinates into his dash, flips two switches, presses a button—and, just like that, his craft vanishes. Where it once hovered, glowing delicately in the hollowness of space, there is no disturbance, no movement or vapor. Only empty blackness.

* * *

The Visitor is standing half-naked on a boardwalk on the western coast of the United States, only a few miles outside Los Angeles. On his feet, he is wearing a rather itchy pair of Velcro-strapped sandals, which chafe with the sand they've accumulated in the brief few moments since he has arrived here. Before him stretches a strip of narrow, yellow beach, sloping toward an immense body of water. He gathers from the conversations of the myriad two-legged beings milling all around him that this water is called the Pacific.

He has thick, shaggy blonde hair, a hooked nose that is more charming than sharp, and aside from the sandals, he is wearing nothing but black swim trunks with red racing stripes. The Visitor is a shape-shifter. The moment he touched down—or, perhaps more accurately, appeared out of thin air—on this swath of tourist beach, he spotted a passing human and shifted into his best imitation of the man's shape.

The Visitor steps down from the boardwalk and begins to walk across the sand. First, his steps are halting. It was fairly easy to mimic the strides of the humans on the hard surface of the boardwalk, but now his feet sink and slide in this infirm substance, this *sand*. But the Visitor is trained to assimilate quickly—to gather observations, catalogue and analyze them, and incorporate them. Within moments, he is gliding across the beach with the ease of a native Californian.

As he moves, he cocks his head, taking in the sounds of the conversations. The majority of the voices follow a clipped, throaty pattern. Here and there, he hears people communicating in different patterns—sometimes more guttural, sometimes sharper, sometimes in opposing tones that collide and bleed into one another. These, he understands, are different languages.

A little boy is constructing an elaborate structure of sand and water near the tide line. The soft lapping of the waves edges closer and closer to the little towers of his creation, but he is unperturbed. He fills a bucket with sand, hardens it with water, then dumps it out to create another tower, which he carefully sculpts with his fingertips.

The Visitor peers down at the little boy. He shields his eyes from the bright glare of the system's star with one hand, as he has seen other humans doing.

After a moment, the boy looks up and meets his gaze. "Hello," he says simply. He, too, speaks the language of the majority of the humans on the beach.

"What are you doing?" the Visitor asks, mimicking the gentle tones he has heard since his arrival, wanting to broadcast, "I mean you no harm." He has near limitless language capabilities and quickly shifts into English.

"Building a castle!" the boy tells him proudly.

The Visitor points at the marauding waves. "The water is destroying it," he says.

The boy shrugs. "I don't care."

"Why not? You are working so hard."

"No, I'm not. I'm just playing."

Just then, a woman in a pink bathing suit and wide-brimmed

straw hat arrives. She takes the boy by the hand. "Time to go, Christopher," she says. The Visitor notes that her tone is stern. As the boy rises, grabbing his bucket with his free hand, the woman catches the Visitor's eye. Her face is a mask of disapproval. She hurries away with the boy, who tosses a wide smile over his shoulder at the Visitor.

The Visitor pauses to integrate these events. *The larger human was the progenitor,* he understands. *And the smaller was the offspring. The young are at ease with outsiders; mature humans appear to consider them threats.*

He lifts his eyes from the sand castle and continues to scan the beach. He studies the groupings of people, the way they interact —and do not interact—with one another. He sees that there are males and females, young and old. He notices that their hair is different lengths, textures, and colors; it reflects the light differently. He sees that some are taller and some are heavier. Some are light-skinned; some are darker. None of these physical details strike him as particularly important, but he notes everything. Observing, after all, is why he has come.

Humans have differences, he understands, *but they are all unmistakably members of the same family.*

* * *

The Visitor continues his journey over this blue marble that he has come to learn is called *Earth* by its dominant inhabitants. He discovers that the same creatures he saw on the beach, humans, populate most of the planet's landmasses. There are millions of other species, but only the humans are capable of reason, complex abstract thought, and language. He sees that they are in control of Earth's resources. In his mental catalogue, he classifies them as *DSDs: Dominant Surface Dwellers.*

    He becomes bolder in his interactions. He discovers that though they are remarkably similar, though they all laugh, cry, work and play, experience fear, and cherish their own children, they have divided the Earth into different territories, and each territory has its own rules and customs. Just after leaving Beijing, in a large territory called China, he tries to bow to a man in the British territory and is met only with confusion. At last, the man extends his hand—and the Visitor understands that it is to be clasped in greeting.

    Different territories, different greetings, the Visitor concludes. *But greeting seems essential.*

    He diplomatically avoids any explanation of who he is or where he has come from. He does not wish to disrupt human activity with his presence. He wants only to observe.

    The Visitor travels and assumes new shapes. He floats with a group of blonde-haired men in a curiously hot natural spring outside of Reykjavik, Iceland. He gathers at a conference table with black-haired, somberly clad men and women at the top of a high-rise in Tokyo, Japan. He squats with a cluster of dreadlocked women stirring a boiling pot of mutton stew at the edge of a Namibian village. He touches his forehead to the ground in an Iranian mosque. He chants a long, breathless *ohm* in a temple in Mumbai. He dances in the aisles of a clapboard church in Mississippi.

    In an ornate auditorium in Tbilisi, Georgia, the Visitor watches from a red velvet seat as ballet dancers whirl on a stage before him. His eyes pass from the audience to the dancers and back again. All around him, people are watching, breathless. Their lips are parted with wonder. The eyes of the woman beside him are moist, and she presses a hand to her heart. When he follows her gaze back to the performance, he sees the bodies of these humans curve elegantly, leaping and spinning with a stunning combination of lightness and strength. He sees that their dance is more than physical accomplishment. He sees that it conveys emotion, story. It is art.

Not long after, the Visitor wanders into a violin shop off a narrow, cobblestone street in Florence. A plump man behind the counter is showing a violin to a young couple. He touches the shining curves of its wood and murmurs a few words about tone. Then he lifts it to his shoulder and brings the bow to the strings. The violin sings. Its notes float with an unmistakable sorrow to the Visitor's ears. He is captivated.

Then, a twinkle enters the violinmaker's eye. He stomps one foot on the ground four times, and suddenly the bow is flying over the strings, the notes jumping from the tiny instrument with more precision than the Visitor would have thought possible. Gone is the sweet sadness of the tune, and in its place is soaring joy—with a hint of mischief. The Visitor is awed. This is music.

Humans are capable of profound expression, he notes. *Their emotional and social life is rich and varied, and they translate it into art and literature. This is more than simple communication. The artist's experience becomes the viewer's. A remarkable achievement. A remarkable species.*

But the Visitor travels long and far. Gradually, experiences that he cannot comprehend begin to overwhelm his impressions of Earth. He huddles with a family in a makeshift shelter in the Paktia Province of Afghanistan, unsure whether the row after row of armed men marching past mean help or harm. He watches as police officers in Chicago unroll a barrier of yellow tape around the driveway where one young man has killed another with a handgun, a weapon these humans have designed to be both deadly and concealable. He stands spellbound before a row of clever machines called televisions as they all simultaneously flash images of debris left by a bomb in a place called the West Bank.

He asks a woman nearby what the images mean. "What happened?" he wants to know.

"Uhm . . ." She gazes at the screens for a moment. "I'm not really sure. Something about the Israelis and the Palestinians fighting again. Listen, if this model doesn't interest you, you can watch these same scenes in high definition. Let me show you our other models."

He stares at her, uncomprehending.

The Visitor sees young men and women chain themselves to an ancient tree in British Columbia, preventing loggers from cutting it down; then he follows the manager of the logging company back to his office trailer and watches him stare with blank despair at a stack of payroll checks he cannot sign. The Visitor stands on the outskirts of a drilling area in Western Australia where men are draining a subterranean water source that will not replenish for centuries; he sees one worker clap another on the back and say, "We won't let this drought beat us." In some circles, he hears people use words like "ozone" and "carbon monoxide" with dread tingeing their voices; in others, he hears the same words spoken with derision.

The Visitor meets a group of people building a school in southern Pakistan. It is simple, but functional, and he can see that it will serve many children well.

"I've seen a place not far from here that needs a school," the Visitor tells one of the group's leaders. He points east.

"Across that ridge?" the woman asks him.

He nods.

She sighs and nods as well. "Sure. But that's across the border. Our grants are for Pakistan."

The Visitor squints at her. He does not understand.

Don't Drink the Water

* * *

Several months, as these humans measure time, have passed. The Visitor sits in a park in Moscow, where a light snow is falling. He relishes the strangeness of this white crystallized water brushing against his cheeks. Not far from him, two young parents are walking, clasping the hands of a little girl between them. She runs for several steps and then jumps, her parents lifting her by the arms so that she swings suspended between them. As soon as they return her to the ground, she runs and jumps again.

The Visitor remembers seeing this game many times before, in places as disparate as Tennessee and Turkey. He cannot help but be charmed by the image of the child soaring, her parents lifting her from the earth.

Such potential, he thinks. But the moment the thought enters his mind, a feeling of despondency overtakes him. From a pocket of the heavy parka he learned quickly to wear in this season called "winter," he extracts a small, black device. He inputs a message.

Observations complete.

Summary: The Dominant Surface Dweller (DSD) is a biped with grasping and imagining capacity. DSD population appears to have grown quickly from initial, inconsequential numbers. Until recently, their effect on Planet #3 was minimal. Population now surpasses six billion. DSDs' current activities will almost certainly destroy Planet #3's life-supporting capacity if continued at present rate. But DSDs also threaten to destroy themselves. They continually develop sophisticated and unsophisticated weaponry, which they turn against themselves when a conflict over beliefs or resources occurs. Some DSDs are aware of the disastrous long-term consequences of their current activities, but as a whole they continue to find justifications for them. Though many will readily acknowledge these justifications as suicidal, most believe that they remain "reasonable."

Planet #3 and its inhabitants have remarkable potential. The DSD capacity to imagine and create has few cosmic rivals. But when it comes to their willingness to justifiably destroy themselves and the surface of their planet, they stand alone. It is difficult to remain in the presence of such self-destruction and such unrealized potential.
Mission concluded.

The Visitor taps a key on his device. It emits a low beep of confirmation. The message has been transmitted. He gives one last glance to his surroundings, watching the backs of the little girl and her parents as they retreat quietly through the snow. Then, with the press of a few buttons, he disappears.

* * *

We are all visitors here.

Earth has been here for four billion years and will remain for about another eight or nine billion—until our sun lives out its lifespan and, its gravity no longer able to contain its energy, explodes. Our arrivals and departures on Earth, and the spans of time they contain, are inconsequentially brief when compared to the many billions of arrivals and departures our host has seen. As individuals, we visit, and we are gone again.

Adopting this perspective, looking at the world through the eyes of a visitor is not as much of a stretch for the human mind as it might at first seem to be. After all, when we are born, we are all fresh, questioning, and untrained. We see without the lens of labels distorting our vision. Then we begin looking to those who have been here longer to learn about our various cultures and how to behave within them. Over time, we are handed the labels our parents were handed, and it becomes our duty to ensure that our children wear those same labels. Where once we were visitors, seeing with our eyes, we are now residents, seeing with our minds what we were taught to see.

We need labels. We have to have a personal relationship with the world around us. Labeling ourselves and everyone else is a tool for communicating our unique histories and perspectives. But what happens when the identifying labels become more important to us than the identified humans? What happens when we see only labels and borders rather than the humanity that is our common family and the earth that is our common home?

As a little boy, when I began to feel the disconnectedness that came with the labels used to divide us, I cried. I did not know then why I was crying, but I did feel a sense of connectedness that was slipping away. And I felt the suffering caused by the loss of that connectedness. At some level, we all feel it; we just learn to accommodate it.

It was not until I sat atop a tower crane, day after day for nine months, looking out across a world where borders are intangible, arbitrary creations, that I began again to feel the visitor within myself. Many years later, I had the same feeling again, only more forcefully, more clearly. On one of my "sabbaticals" to the Adirondacks, I stepped out into the river one morning after I had been alone in the woods for five days. As I floated on my back in the chill, autumn water, staring up at the canopy of trees and hearing nothing but the whispering silence of the wilderness, I realized that these mountains had been this way for millennia, unchanged by the small blips in time that visitors like me represent. I was temporary; the Adirondacks were timeless.

And then I understood. Out there, far from the rush, the jobs, the houses, the highways, the *culture* that asks us to define ourselves, I could be anyone. Of course, at birth, like everyone else, I had been handed labels—but their geographical and historical allotment was arbitrary. I could have been born in any place and at any time, and the labels would have been different. Suddenly, I became aware of the timelessness of being human and the temporariness of being *a* human. For the second time in my life, I was seeing the world without looking through the lens of labels. I was a visitor again.

For the rest of my stay in the Adirondacks, I thought about us as a visitor might. A visitor could not help but notice that we are goal-oriented, but that the goal of our collective, long-term survival has yet to be established.

As soon as I was back in range of cell service, I called my friend Paul.

"I'm going to talk," I told him. "I've got something to say."

Much of my story, as you have read, has been about gaining the confidence to start talking. It has been about learning that, yes, an average American citizen can have an opinion about the future of our world.

And I hope you'll join me in that sense of confidence. It's not a stretch for average citizens to adopt the perspective of visitors, to set aside, however briefly, the lens of labels and think together about our shared future. If that kind of thinking were impossible, I wouldn't be here, writing this book. And if I can do it, any one of us can.

So, for the rest of this book, walk out on a limb with me. Let's reject the line of thinking that tells us that human beings are fatally flawed, that it's just not in our nature, not in our brain capacity, to adopt a global, long-term perspective. If only for a day, for an hour, for a few moments . . . what if we look with a sense of newness at our home? What would we see?

And what would we do about it?

Chapter Thirteen

The very triumph of scientific annihilation has destroyed the possibility of war being a medium of practical settlement of international differences . . . If you lose, you are annihilated. If you win, you stand only to lose. War contains the germs of double suicide . . . Military alliances, balances of power, leagues of nations all in turn have failed . . . We have our last chance. If we will not devise some greater and more equitable system, Armageddon will be at our door.
—General Douglas MacArthur

Unfortunately, I cannot aim to describe with anything approaching completeness what a visitor might see here on Earth. I could spend the rest of my life, and the rest of the lives of a team of assistants, trying to outline every last human and environmental injustice that would become obvious to any observer unwilling to use the mental escapes of accommodating or simply ignoring. We would fill volumes. By the time we thought we'd finished, a new edition would be long overdue. We'd have to begin again, cataloguing, inventorying, tallying up the many ways in which current human activity has placed us on a collision course with ourselves.

And ultimately, such a cataloguing would be futile. We already know the countless ways in which we are failing. We know them, and we accommodate them, because we believe them to be inevitable and irreparable.

So, rather than trying to give you a complete picture of the threats to our collective survival that we are currently facing, let me start with one small thread. A representative sample. All I have to do is open the morning paper, on any morning, in any city or town on the planet, and I'll find enough examples to let the wind out of even the sturdiest of sails.

On the morning of this writing alone, the World section of the *New York Times* led with headlines on no fewer than eight armed conflicts. The United States and Afghanistan. The United States and Iraq. Britain and Afghanistan. Ethnic Uzbeks and Kyrgyzstan. Ethnic Kurds and Turkey. An international terrorist organization and national governments. Thai dissidents and the Thai government. Israel and Palestine.

Every day we accommodate these and countless other conflicts. We have to, to get past the morning paper and on to our morning coffee and morning commute. We tell ourselves, "These conflicts are inevitable," or, "There's nothing I can do about this." We close the paper and move on; we search for other ways to fill the sense of human disconnectedness that haunts us.

What if, just for the time it takes to read this chapter, we let a single one of those eight conflicts really permeate our consciousness? Say we pick Israel and Palestine.

Ask the average American citizen on the street what is at the heart of the conflict between Israel and Palestine, and you'll most likely hear land or perhaps simply religion. But what about water? The article in this morning's paper discusses basic resources that are in contention between the two territories. And chief among them is water.

Today, we take up arms for oil. Now imagine if the nonrenewable resource at issue weren't one like oil or coal that simply yields comfort and convenience. What if it were one that we need to live? What if it were water?

One of my friends from the cafeteria table at Canisius went on to earn a degree in mathematics and work for the US Army Corps of Engineers. There, he developed a computer program that he now uses all over the world as a private consultant to assist in resolving water disputes. He can input all the players in a dispute, anyone even peripherally dependent on the water source in question, and work toward an equitable solution for distributing the water.

His lifetime of research has convinced him that the most contentious issue for our children will be neither oil nor coal. It will be water. At this very moment, all over the world, we are draining aquifers deep underground. Unlike shallow wells, they do not replenish relatively quickly with the change of seasons. These aquifers take several generations to fill again, yet we are emptying them for crop and cattle production that will feed only the current generation.

Now let's return to that article in today's paper. What we don't often hear discussed is that there are two aquifers directly below the Green Line that separates the Israeli and Palestinian territories—and who has the right to drill for the water in them is a matter of basic survival in the arid Middle East.

This particular dispute, however, is one example among many. Where there is no equitable, enforceable system for determining the allocation of resources with intelligence, the contention has to be resolved somehow. When the resources mean the difference between poverty and prosperity, between even life and death, it is human nature to try every avenue open to claim those resources. We are wired, individually, to survive—even if at our collective peril. And so when the only avenue open is to take up arms, we will.

In 2003, Virginia developers and planners warned the state

government that a water crisis was imminent. The Washington, DC suburbs in Northern Virginia were booming, and the water systems in place at the time could not meet the demand. The Virginia water supply experts came up with the solution of installing an intake in the Potomac River, which separates Virginia from Maryland. The catch was that because of the seasonal rising and falling of the Potomac water level, the intake had to be placed in the center of the river, at the water's deepest, so that it would always remain submerged in any season. Maryland took issue: it owns the Potomac River right up to the Virginia shore.

Virginia brought its case against Maryland to the Supreme Court, and the Supreme Court ruled in its favor. Both parties had agreed before walking into the courtroom—in fact, had agreed for centuries, simply by entering into the federation that is the United States of America—to honor the decision of the Court. Today, there is an intake in the middle of the Potomac that serves Northern Virginia.

What if there were no Supreme Court? Or what if its rulings were neither binding nor enforceable? It's no stretch to imagine a scenario in which the border between Maryland and Virginia looked like the Green Line.

Human beings will always wield tools to our advantage. Where there is a problem, we search for the right tool to fix it. And this has meant, throughout history, that we have applied the tool of weaponry to the problem of unresolved disputes. From bows and arrows to swords to guns to tanks to remote-controlled bomber planes, we are continually seeking to obtain better and better tools.

Today, the most powerful tool we have is the nuclear bomb. And because nuclear bombs are so destructive, all the countries that already possess them have gotten together and declared, "For our own safety, for the safety of the planet, no one else can have this weapon." But for the countries lacking nuclear weapons, that doesn't sound like an equitable plan. To protect themselves, they want to be able to threaten their enemies with obliteration, too. Their desire creates a market; and as any businessman knows, whether he sells insurance policies or deals in the black market weapons trade: where there is a market, there is a way. Someone will meet the need and sell that weapon.

We call this process an "arms race." But what's really going on is a fear race. Whichever country or group controls the most powerful weapons also controls their enemies by keeping them in fear of the use of those weapons. Using fear as stock in trade is no secret, either. When the United States invaded Iraq in 2003, its expressed intent was to "shock and awe" the Iraqi citizenry into submission. When I first heard the phrase, I was left speechless by its darkness. We couch this darkness in clinical, strategic terms, but the living, breathing, human ramification is *fear*.

Naturally, weaker countries do not want to be slaves to fear. They want the playing field leveled—they want to hold stock in fear, too. And so, while a wealthy player in the international race might keep its enemies in fear of its nuclear power, a poorer player might keep its enemies in fear of terrorist attacks. There is no finish line in the fear race. It is a perpetual game of one-upmanship.

And it doesn't work. Fear attacks the symptom: it silences, through force, those who disagree with us or those who hold the resources we want. To return to the example of Virginia and Maryland's water dispute, imagine if Virginia's leaders decided to strike fear into the hearts of Maryland's citizens. Imagine if they used weaponry to force the leaders of Maryland to give up their rights to the waters of the Potomac. The tenuous peace would hold only until Maryland had rebuilt its infrastructure and restocked its weapons. And in the intervening years, the fervor of the families left broken and impoverished by Virginia's bombs would only grow. Continually living in fear leads to anger, which leads to hatred, which breeds violence. There might be no end in sight to the great Virginia/Maryland water war.

It used to be that one tribe attacked another tribe, one city-state attacked another city-state, or one nation attacked another nation. And this system of resolution, though never efficient and often self-perpetuating, was at least self-contained. The goal was to conquer the enemy, and that was possible. Today's conflicts are no longer so neatly contained; there is no one to declare, "We surrender." The United States, in its unique position as the world's sole remaining superpower and in possession of the world's largest military, will not surrender. No nation possessing nuclear capabilities will surrender. And no nation or group fighting with God on its side will surrender. The goal of warfare in this context can no longer be to conquer; it has to be to destroy outright. To obliterate. And so our leaders now tell us we will have to learn to accommodate a perpetual state of war.

The tool no longer fits the problem. Our disputes are too diffuse and too borderless for weaponry to resolve them. So we learn to accommodate, by taking our shoes off at the airport and by living in a world labeled "code orange." On one side, we are bombarded with news and images that tell us we are losing ground, and on the other, we are told by our leaders that rather than finding a new approach to settling human disputes, the answer is to funnel more resources, more time, more lives into the tools that are currently failing.

***

That's what a visitor would see, looking at Earth. A world where the current system for resolving disputes only perpetuates them. And this is the perspective that arose from one article in one newspaper on one morning. This is one sliver of the panorama that would await us, if we chose to remove the labels from our eyes. Had I picked up the *LA Times* rather than the *New York Times*, had I watched the news rather than reading the paper, this chapter might contain a different sliver—but one no less grim.

And this is precisely why we avoid the visitor's perspective: because if we lived as visitors in every moment, we wouldn't be able to read even a one-column article in the morning paper without despairing, without wondering, "Why?" Our alternative is to accommodate by taking solace in the labels that divide us. We say, "Well. That article is about the Middle East. I can't get upset over the whole wide world."

And in a hopeless world, we'd be right to say so. If we're losing ground every day, and we see evidence of it everywhere we turn, we have to learn to shut it out somehow. But what if we didn't believe ourselves to be irreparably, inherently flawed? Accommodation is only necessary if you believe that we human beings are the way we are because we have no other way to be.

The species that we call the "modern human"—*our* species—is only about two hundred and fifty thousand years old. Now, if we were to say, very roughly, that a new generation of humans arrives on the planet every twenty-five years, then ten thousand generations existed before us. About nine thousand three hundred and seventy-five of those generations never saw a printed page. Only the last four generations have experienced flight. Only the last two have used a computer. And only one generation—ours—has had the communications technology to develop a perspective of global awareness. We have a new perspective that nine thousand nine hundred and ninety-nine generations did not have. We are the first generation to be aware of the suicidal nature of current human activity, and how we react to our newfound awareness will impact all future generations.

If we play our cards right, and it is the explosion of the sun rather than the explosion of a nuclear bomb that marks the end of our species . . . ten thousand generations existed before us, and *three hundred and twenty million generations* will exist after us.

We are so young. We are in our adolescence. And, like teenagers, we are self-occupied—we think the world turns on our axis. We rush into the kitchen, grab everything out of the fridge, and eat without stopping to wonder who went to the grocery store, who prepared the food, and who will wash our dirty dishes. Over time, parents teach their teenagers to do these things on their own, to appreciate the sources of their sustenance and the consequences of their actions. And, like teenagers, we too will learn to take note of these things, and we will learn to take care of ourselves and those who will follow us. We will learn that the world turns on its own axis, not on ours. But unlike teenagers, we will have to teach ourselves.

If you measure a teenager's progress by comparing him to his childhood self, it's plain to see that he's taken leaps and bounds. He used to crawl across the living room; now he can dribble a ball down the basketball court. He used to babble; now he can tell jokes, sing songs, make a logical argument. He used to scribble with crayons; now he can write an essay. But what if you used a different yardstick to measure his progress? Rather than checking his progress against his past, what if you checked it against his potential?

Now you might see a different picture. Knowing that someday he could become the CEO of a corporation, a kindergarten teacher, an orthopedic surgeon, or a father . . . you gain a new perspective on his progress. This doesn't mean that his accomplishments thus far are suddenly worthless—but it does mean that you can now see clearly that he's not finished yet.

When it comes to measuring individual progress, we're fascinated by potential. We hear teachers say all the time, "Your child's got such potential." We talk about giving our kids opportunities and protecting their progress because we believe so firmly that they're on a path, and we want them to continue as far down it as they can. But, strangely, we never think about potential when it comes to measuring our collective, human progress. Instead, we tell ourselves, "We used to fight with sticks and clubs; we used to cook on open fires; we used to let sewage run down the streets." We say, "See how far we've come?" And we consider ourselves finished.

But what if we started measuring human intelligence against the yardstick of our potential? Suddenly, our understanding of ourselves and the path we're on would broaden exponentially. We would see that we have not arrived at our destination. We would see that we are very young and that we have the potential to grow beyond our experience—that we are evolving.

Imagine how we would feel about ourselves if our generation took the next step in the evolution of human intelligence. Imagine how we would feel if we set the first goal—the goal that will make all other goals for the future of humanity possible. If we set the goal, simply put, to stop killing each other. What if we aimed to "shock and awe" the world not with our ability to instill fear, but with our intelligence and compassion? With our commitment to finding a new, more intelligent way of resolving our national and religious disputes? Imagine the resources, the time, the energy, the lives that would be freed up. Just as H.G. Wells wrote, it would "mean such a release and increase in human energy as to open up a new phase in human history."

On the day after our national leaders gather together and expressly state their commitment to the goal of *creating an intelligent alternative to weaponry for settling national and religious disputes* . . . imagine what it will feel like to be human.

Chapter Fourteen

Details are not crucial; the important point is to find a plan . . . that would be both effective and generally acceptable. If a sufficient effort is made, the effective wisdom of mankind can find the right combination.
—Louis Sohn, *World Peace Through World Law*

Establishing the goal of creating an intelligent alternative to weaponry for settling disputes is a mandatory starting point. We cannot accomplish anything under the cloud of war. But what other goals remain to be set? What other areas need our collective attention—what's the next step in the ongoing evolution of our intelligence?

We do not have a sustainable relationship with our environment.

Full stop.

In a truly logical world, this chapter would end here. *We do not have a sustainable relationship with our environment.* Our current practices *will* eventually end—either because we exhaust Earth's life-supporting capacity, or because we set another goal: creating a sustainable relationship with our home planet.

Just as I could not sketch the details of every last armed conflict on Earth in the previous chapter, I am not able to catalogue every last way in which our current means of production and consumption are at odds with our environment. But, again, let's take a look at a small sliver of the picture.

In 2004, I found a tool that could give the average person the visitor's perspective on the world. During my work with Global Plan Initiative, I came across an organization called Sustainable Resources, which was planning an international conference at the University of Colorado, Boulder. After flying to Boulder to meet with the executive director of Sustainable Resources, Steve Troy, I was sure that there was synergy between what he was doing and what I was doing. GPI became a main sponsor of the conference.

As soon as we had finalized GPI's participation, an image popped into my mind. Some time earlier, just by chance, I had seen a Mark Trail comic strip in the Sunday *Washington Post*. I don't even read Mark Trail comics, but this one had somehow jumped out at me. The comic strip was about an actual scientific development created by the National Oceanic and Atmospheric Administration (NOAA). Researchers there had created the technology necessary to project onto a sphere, rather than on a flat surface. The result was an exact replica of Earth, a large spherical movie screen capable of giving the viewer a real-time astronaut's perspective, complete with moving projections of the continents and weather systems. The globe could be used to show what Earth had looked like millions of years ago, how it looks at this moment—and also how it might look in the future. NOAA had named the globe Science On a Sphere.

I called NOAA to ask about including Science On a Sphere in the Sustainable Resources Conference.

"I'm involved in planning a conference on sustainability," I told the NOAA representative who answered the phone. "I think your sphere would be a great addition. Have you ever moved it to a different location?"

"We have," she said. "As a matter of fact, we just took it to Sea Island, Georgia, for the G8 conference."

"How much did that cost?"

"Fifty thousand dollars."

Well, that was effectively the end of that conversation. Fifty thousand dollars was no problem for the eight wealthiest nations in the world, but it was a big problem for GPI. I hung up the phone thinking that this was a missed opportunity.

But then the scrap of paper where I'd jotted down the NOAA phone number caught my eye. It was the same area code as Steve Troy's phone number.

I redialed.

"How far are you from the University of Colorado?" I asked.

"We're five minutes away."

And that's how, on the last day of the Sustainable Resources Conference, 120 of the conference sponsors and speakers gathered at the NOAA facilities to view the Earth as visitors. Among those in attendance was Dr. Sandy MacDonald, then the director of NOAA's Forecast Systems Laboratory, and the inventor of Science On a Sphere. He had spent many hours in his garage working on developing the technology necessary to project on a sphere because he had a message that he wanted to share. He knew from his research and the research of hundreds if not thousands of his colleagues that current human activity is unsustainable and in the end suicidal—a simple message. And he wanted to find a way to communicate that message in universities, schools, museums— wherever people were willing to listen and engage. The answer he came up with was Science On a Sphere.

Consistently, astronauts returning from missions to space use the word "transformative." One day, they are on solid ground, the people and the places of their lives so close and so engaging as to be invisible. And the next, they are in outer space. Before them is a sphere, blue, white, and green, suspended against an infinite blackness. Perhaps for the first time, they understand this sphere to be their home. They know it is the place they stood on mere hours ago. And yet here it is before them, so majestic, so beautiful, and so wondrously alive.

In groups of thirty, we went to the basement of the building to see it. We entered the darkened room, and spread out in a circle. Then, before our eyes, Earth appeared out of the blackness.

NOAA has coined the term the "blue marble" for our world as it appears in space. And that's exactly what we were looking at. There was Earth, blue and smooth as a marble. We were seeing exactly what a visitor approaching the planet from afar would see. It was a fascinating, and for some, transformative sight.

NOAA researchers went on to share a visual presentation on how Earth had come to be as it is today. As we watched, we saw the continents as they were millions of years ago—one solid landmass called Pangaea. A small, illuminated dot in the northwestern corner of the landmass appeared. This was the place that would, six hundred million years later, be dubbed Indiana.

We watched as the continents separated and drifted outward until, slowly, before our eyes, we saw something recognizable coalesce. There was Asia, and there Europe. And there was North America, with an illuminated portion below the Great Lakes representing a far more familiar Indiana—still continuing to move at the same pace as it has for six hundred million years.

But the image did not freeze there. The NOAA researchers went on to show us projections into the future, images of how human activity is changing weather systems and how those changes are affecting our planet.

"This is Earth only fifty years from now," they told us. "Some of us in this room may still be alive to see this. Many of our children will almost certainly witness it."

A great swath of land across northern Canada slowly darkened from green to brown. The colors represented the warming earth, with the deep brown corresponding to temperatures twenty to thirty degrees Fahrenheit warmer than today.

We glanced around the room at each other, shifting our weight awkwardly, unsure how to digest this information. There we were, in direct contact with the best scientists our tax dollars could afford. As citizens, we had effectively hired them and tasked their organization, NOAA, with advising us on matters of the environment. It was one thing for us to read in the comfort of our own homes that nameless, faceless researchers working in some unknown lab and churning out mysterious studies were warning of catastrophe. It was quite another to share a space with those researchers, to know that they are the best we've got doing the best they can.

Their best work has produced this very simple message: human activity is on an accelerating suicidal course. Somehow, when this message leaves the walls of NOAA's labs and passes through our many cultural filters, it changes in the public conversation from a fact to an opinion. But that day, looking at that globe, we could not call it opinion. We pay the salaries of these scientists to do research and advise us, and as we stood in the NOAA basement, watching the only home we have change irreparably before our eyes, their message was clear. Every hour of every day, we are destroying our own life-support systems.

For that one evening, we joined the NOAA researchers as visitors to planet Earth. And what we saw was dark.

But the projections on that globe weren't carved in stone. Imagine we have the potential to end our dependence on nonrenewable energy and begin the era of sustainability. And imagine if we could start by setting one goal. On the day after our national leaders, with one voice, declare their commitment to the goal of *developing a completely sustainable relationship with the environment* . . . imagine what it will feel like to be human.

* * *

We've now set two goals for the collective future of humanity. What's left? In a world where we can guarantee our children a method for settling disputes with dignity and intelligence, and in a world where we hand our children our declared commitment to sustainability . . . how could we channel our newly liberated time and resources into the continual evolution of human intelligence?

What do we owe the future inhabitants of the earth?

It might seem at first like an esoteric question, something for academics to debate in their ivory tower, far from our immediate need to stay safe and warm, make money, raise our children. But rather than wondering about faceless future inhabitants, what if we think about the very next inhabitants of the earth, those who will immediately follow us?

What do we owe our children? For those of us who have children, our answer is almost universally, "Quite a lot." We owe them food, clothing, shelter, an education. We owe them consolation when they are hurt or frightened. We owe them shared joy in their triumphs. We owe them love. And even if we are not parents ourselves, we willingly accept some portion of the responsibility for the next generation. We pay taxes so that all children can go to school and to the doctor. Some form of this shared responsibility exists in every nation in the world. In every single culture, humans rally around their children to support and protect them.

Now what about the children of our children? Many of us will live long enough to know our grandchildren personally, to hold their bottles and their hands, to pick them up from school, to be amazed at their crayon drawings or their batting averages. Do we owe them any less, because they are one generation removed, than what we owed our children before them?

What if we live long enough to know our grandchildren's children? Would we say then, "Okay, this is where I draw the line. I've fulfilled my responsibility to my children and grandchildren; *this* generation is on its own."

That's exactly the statement we're making today, in gestures small and large, from the flick of a wrist it takes to toss a plastic water bottle into the garbage to the mammoth case of collective accommodation it takes to sign on as a nation to a state of perpetual warfare. We are using our current concept of time to create an artificial end to our intergenerational responsibilities.

Teaching our children, as we were taught, that there will always be victims of poverty, hunger, illiteracy, and preventable disease is a self-perpetuating lesson that limits our and their potential. We would never silently bear witness to our own children's suffering, but every day, we tolerate circumstances that will result in our children's children's suffering. We tolerate them because it has become acceptable to believe that there is no end in sight to human injustice; it has become acceptable to believe that we have no other choice. Like teenagers who raid the fridge without a second thought to the before and after of their actions, we live without any truly developed sense of *intergenerational justice*.

We're used to thinking of justice as being bound by the limitations of time and space. There must be a perpetrator and a victim, and they have to have shared a moment and place in time. We even put a statute of limitations on justice so that we can't go accusing each other of long-forgotten crimes. But just as the concepts in this book call on us to expand our awareness in the *physical dimension*, to start looking at the ramifications of our actions beyond our own borders, we also have to start expanding our awareness in the *temporal dimension*.

Until the Industrial Revolution a century and a half ago, human activity had containable consequences. There was no reason to wonder about intergenerational responsibility because farms were too small to alter the landscape, the smoke from wood stoves and fires was negligible, and wars fought with swords and even muskets eventually ended.

As we have seen in the last two chapters, however, the parameters today have changed drastically. Our technology means that for the first time in history, the ramifications of our actions—from detonating bombs in city squares to spilling oil in the oceans—are no longer bound by national borders. And they are no longer bound by years or decades, either. We can no more constrain the effects of our actions to our own lifetimes as we can expect a cloud of smog created by a plant in China to hover above China forever, perpetually contained by national borders even in the atmosphere.

Where there is a victim of human activity, whether in the immediate or in the future, there has been an injustice. And where there has been an injustice, restoring justice is the goal. But today's new parameters call for a revision of our definition of justice—they call for us to take intergenerational justice into account when we decide how we are going to conduct ourselves.

Imagine, then, a world where we take the coming generations into account. What goal would we set for them? On the day after our world leaders affirm their commitment to *creating an effective method for addressing and eventually eliminating poverty, hunger, illiteracy, and all deaths from diseases with known cures* . . . imagine what it will feel like to be human.

* * *

One day, a few years after September 11, I found myself sitting under a tree in the woods wondering, "What do I *want?*" Already, my wife and friends had begun to chafe at my preoccupation with research. I had found a hundred different ways to state the problem at hand, but everyone around me was saying, "Okay, okay, we get it. But so what? There's nothing to be done." I couldn't back off; I couldn't drop it. I was convinced that there *was* something to be done.

And so, alone in one of my many "outdoor offices," I asked myself, "What do I want? What would make the crying stop? What would make me breathe easy and say, 'We've overcome the disconnectedness. We're now all on the same page.'?"

I didn't have to wonder for more than ten minutes. As soon as I asked myself out loud, the three goals I have outlined in the previous chapter and in this one became obvious. And since the moment when I first articulated these goals for myself, they have not changed in my mind. I have found that I have neither had to add to them, nor take anything away. If we call upon our world leaders to hold a global summit with the professed intention of reorganizing humanity on the macro level so that we can better work together toward achieving these three goals, we will have done justice for future generations and for our own.

And if we do not set these goals? Imagine a court of intergenerational justice where today's generation stands accused of criminal negligence toward future generations. As in any other fair and balanced legal proceeding, we would have the right to a vigorous defense—and future generations, too, would have the right to a vigorous prosecution. If today's best attorneys stood up as proxies for future generations, would they conclude that our generation has knowingly persisted in activities that will have adverse consequences for those to follow us? What evidence could our defense attorneys call upon to say we haven't?

Why not give our attorneys Exhibit A? Imagine them stepping before the bench and submitting a document drawn up at a global summit of all of today's national leaders, signed by every one of them—without a single dissenting vote.

> *To ensure the continual human habitation of the planet Earth in a civilized and sustainable manner, we do hereby adopt the following long-term goals for humanity: (1) the creation of an intelligent alternative to weaponry to settle national and religious disputes; (2) the development of a completely sustainable relationship with the environment; and (3) the creation of the tools necessary to effectively address and eventually eliminate poverty, hunger, illiteracy, and all deaths from diseases with known cures.*
>
> *We are adopting the above goals to reflect our current concept of intergenerational justice. We understand that achieving these long-term goals will take time, but today we are taking the first step. We are committed to creating a plan, document, or organization that will allow us to focus our attention on accomplishing humanity's long-term goals.*

With that document entered into evidence, the defense could rest with a lot more confidence.

Were we actually on trial, I believe the deciding factor in our guilt or innocence would not be whether or not we have *accomplished* those three goals. It would be whether or not we've set them.

Don't Drink the Water

When a child is born, her parents don't demand of themselves that they fill her college savings account that very day, but they *do* open the account. Perhaps it will be filled by the time she is three days old; perhaps it won't be filled until the day she registers for college classes. But it will certainly never be filled if they don't open it.

What is required today for the health of our species is not that we resolve all our problems in an instant . . . it's that we collectively agree to resolve them. And do you think we could agree? It's true that when we open the paper or turn on the news, we're greeted with a barrage of evidence to the contrary, statements about humanity that tell us, "We're too different. We're too self-absorbed. Agreeing on universal goals will never happen in my lifetime, so why bother?"

But do you think, someday, somewhere in the future, we could all agree that humans could come up with another way of resolving disputes besides killing each other? Not tomorrow, but someday.

If you think we can, then that's one long-term goal we can agree to work on together.

And do you think we could all agree that someday we could have a sustainable relationship with the environment?

Well, that's goal number two.

And by the same token, do you think we could all agree that someday every one of our children will have access to life's basic necessities?

There's goal number three.

Acting with justice toward ourselves and future generations does not mean agreeing on everything; it means agreeing on three basic, universal goals. And it does not mean achieving those goals tomorrow; it simply means setting them today.

On the day the President of the United States sits down with the Prime Minister of Russia, the Supreme Leader of Iran, the Federal Council of Switzerland, the Premier of China, and every other head of government of every other nation and signs a document outlining our common, human goals . . . no practical facts of life will change for any human being.

But the way we feel about being human will never be the same.

Chapter Fifteen

If we fail to seize the moment, history will never forgive us.
—Thomas J. Watson Jr.,
Former Ambassador to the Soviet Union

We've identified three common, long-term goals. Three goals that would, if adopted, put us all on the same page for the first time in our brief history. Three goals that would free up enough energy, time, and resources to usher in a new era of human creativity. Three goals that would, simply put, change what it means to be human.

But I've found that, when discussing these goals with other citizens, simply stating them isn't enough. Everyone has questions—and many have objections. In this chapter, I'll list the questions and objections I most often hear, and I'll share the responses my experience and research have led me to.

We've held summits before—and they haven't changed much. What makes you think this one will be any different?

We *have* held summits before. But of all the hundreds and perhaps thousands of international summits that have been held in human history, only two were anything like the one I am suggesting.

The first of these was a regional summit held in Philadelphia in 1787 that ultimately established the Constitution of the United States of America. The second was a global summit held in San Francisco in 1945 that gave rise to the United Nations Charter. Both of these summits were what I would call *rule-changing summits*. The delegates in attendance arrived in the wake of major wars, and with recovery from the devastation of those wars in mind, their task was to write a new set of rules to guide the citizens they represented. The Constitutional Convention in Philadelphia was a resounding success . . . and the United Nations Conference on International Organization has proved, over time, to have been considerably less effective.

I am now suggesting that we make a third effort at a rule-changing summit. And because changing the rules will be the primary objective, this summit will be different from the many ad-hoc, narrowly focused summits we are used to witnessing. The overwhelming majority of international summits are called after a crisis. Perhaps it's financial, perhaps it's military, perhaps it's environmental. Something disrupts or even destroys lives, something that crosses international borders, and our leaders declare, "We must send representatives to find a solution!"

But they also hand those representatives a caveat. While their stated goal is to find a collective solution, they must first and foremost protect the special interests of the citizens and nations they represent. They are instructed to achieve two incompatible objectives: fix the problem and make sure we don't have to change anything. So they arrive at the summit with their hands tied. First, they can only respond retroactively to adverse events that have already taken place, and second, they cannot compromise our national sovereignty in the search for a solution—which, at a summit of multiple independent nations with competing interests, is essentially like saying that they can talk, but they cannot walk the talk.

A rule-changing summit, on the other hand, would allow delegates the freedom necessary to problem solve. While we're used to seeing summits called to discuss our past and how to respond to it, this one would be about discussing our future and how to prepare for it. And while our past summit representatives were guided by the short-term goals of our respective nations, at this summit, the top goal would be the long-term health of the entire human race.

Fortunately for us, we have one successful precedent for this type of summit. The Constitutional Convention is a great example of how the creative use of human intelligence can reorganize human activity. The United States of America did not easily and smoothly spring into being after the Declaration of Independence was signed in 1776 and the Revolutionary War was fought and won. When the war ended, there were thirteen sovereign states, all with competing interests, governments, and currencies. The disorganization was so great that, as Norman Cousins writes, "The value of a citizen's currency would shrink 10 percent when he or she crossed a state line. Thus a citizen who started out from New Hampshire with $100 in his pocket would have $20.24 left by the time he arrived in Georgia—without having spent a cent." It was not until 1788, twelve years—and much discussion, revision, and compromise—after the Revolution that intelligence prevailed, the Constitution was ratified, and unity was achieved.

And how did the states go from disorganization, competition, and even threats of war between themselves to becoming the single most stable, free, and prosperous republic in history? A rule-changing summit. Previous attempts at unifying the states had failed because the delegates were not allowed to compromise in any way. But at the Constitutional Convention in 1787, there were no caveats; the well-being of all was the goal. Over the course of their negotiations, the delegates came up with a new set of rules: a system of checks and balances using the three branches of government that we all memorize so faithfully in elementary school.

And, still, that wasn't the be-all and end-all. The delegates had no right to enforce and ratify their creation. They were simply the best diplomatic minds of the times, tasked with creating an organizational structure, and when they'd settled on it, they had to convince their constituents to accept their creation and the idea that their self-interests could best be served by reorganizing themselves. The Federalist Papers were essentially an effort to persuade the people to adopt the Constitution and create a new border, *a border that encircled all the citizens of every state.*

The people responded with their fears and concerns, and out of those fears, the Bill of Rights was born. The back and forth took time, care, and negotiation—and more than once, what we now know of and take for granted as the United States of America stood perilously close to remaining a loose association of thirteen warlike and economically vulnerable nations. In the end, we took another step forward in the ongoing evolution of our organizing capacity.

We now stand on a similar precipice—and a global summit could draw us away from it. As Nelson A. Rockefeller writes in *The Future of Federalism*, "The federal idea, which our Founding Fathers applied in their historical act of political creation in the eighteenth century, can be applied in this . . . century in the larger context of the world of free nations—if we will but match our forefathers in courage and vision." It's time for a new border, *a border that encircles the citizens of every nation.*

Will we have to give up any national sovereignty?
Yes, we will. And so will the citizens of every other nation. But we will not have to relinquish *all* sovereignty. As Golda Meir, former Prime Minister of Israel, said: "Internationalism does not mean the end of individual nations. Orchestras don't mean the end of violins."

We've done it before. A major stumbling block to ratifying the Constitution of the United States was that the citizens of Delaware, the smallest of the states, feared getting steamrolled by the interests of large states like New York. It was a legitimate concern—but the citizens of New York had their own equally legitimate concern. They wanted enough congressional representation to ensure that their large and diverse population would be provided for. And so an ingenious compromise was devised. Two houses of congress: the Senate, where all states would have equal representation, and the House of Representatives, where representation would be determined by population.

Delaware had to cede some self-determination by accepting that it would have a smaller voice in the House. And New York, too, had to yield in its position by accepting that in the Senate, Delaware's voice would be equal to its own.

People fear that "giving up some national sovereignty" would mean that suddenly the Chinese would have the right to make decisions on local matters in Utah. Or that we would all cede power to some kind of world monarch or ruling class. But I'm not talking about a black-and-white choice between the current status quo and a single, dictatorial global government— obviously both of those choices are untenable. There's a lot of middle ground between those two extremes, and a global summit could help us find it.

Relinquishing some national sovereignty does not mean being

unpatriotic or disrespectful to our nation or our military. In fact, I've always considered the three goals to be deeply patriotic. They are rooted in the ideals on which our country was founded. They do not threaten those ideals—they extend them. And our forefathers knew the time for evolution would come; that's why they gave us the powerful and seriously underutilized tool of the constitutional convention approach to amending our Constitution. They had the wisdom to put power in the hands of the citizens when our future depends on it. But we must choose to use it.

The threats to our survival are now great enough that any one nation cannot overcome them on its own. War, environmental destruction, poverty, hunger, and illiteracy are all problems without passports. It is not wisdom or spiritual enlightenment but common sense that leads one to conclude: global problems require global solutions. And global solutions require global cooperation.

Yes, the citizens of every nation will have to give up some amount of national sovereignty. But the gains for ourselves and for all future generations will make any personal or national sacrifice more than worth it. Our leaders have yet to understand that we, like our ancestors in their times of need, are willing to sacrifice—as long as we know the sacrifices are evenly distributed.

The livelihoods of decent, hardworking people depend on industries that this idea will alter. What will happen to them?

When I was growing up in Buffalo, there was an immense steel plant just outside the city limits on the shores of Lake Erie. It was owned by the Bethlehem Steel Corporation, which at one time was an almost ubiquitous symbol of American industry. The plant had existed in one form or another for over a century, and when I was a boy, the factory covered over fifteen hundred acres. The company more or less built up the "plant town" of

Lackawanna to house its thousands of workers.

When I was working on and off as an oiler in construction, I often joined my dad for jobs at Bethlehem Steel. It was a teeming, breathing organism, filled with heat and smoke and men at work. And then, gradually, it curled in on itself and died. There were a lot of factors involved—the decline of industrial manufacturing in the United States, the availability of cheap steel overseas, management mistakes. Whatever the reason, Bethlehem Steel became outdated. And without a transition, without retraining, reeducation, or guidance, twenty-five thousand employees were released to catch as catch can.

When our national leaders gather together to decide on a new path for humanity, we simply cannot afford to follow in the footsteps of Bethlehem Steel. There are people whose livelihood depends on manufacturing weaponry. There are people employed in industries dependent on unsustainable forms of energy. We cannot brush aside their concerns. Any plan for achieving the three goals I've outlined must include a transition period. Those who have helped our society achieve its past goals—from military to economic supremacy—must be included in the plan for achieving our new goals. We will need both their support and their skills.

On my last visit to upstate New York, I drove along the shore of Lake Erie toward Buffalo. As I rounded a bend, something caught my eye just above the treetops ahead. The white blades of windmills. There were eight electricity-generating windmills built on the empty site of Bethlehem Steel. It was a ghost town of unused smoke stacks and rusting railroad tracks, but there, turning gently above a field of steel slag, were environmentally friendly wind turbines. The people of Buffalo had found a way to repurpose the Bethlehem Steel site, even on grounds rendered unusable by chemical waste. I learned later that the windmill project had been partly led by Lackawanna's mayor—a former Bethlehem employee laid off when the company went under.

Human beings are resilient and constantly adapting to changing circumstances, but any solution that does not include the needs of all of us is not a solution. We can all walk forward together—without leaving anyone behind.

There are too many powerful special interest groups who will block change.

As I learned years ago when I worked to change the development plan of Til Hazel and his colleagues for the Vienna metro station, there will always be powerful special interests. If we use the existence of powerful people or groups as an excuse for not making a change, then change will never happen. There will never come a time when there are no special interests counting on "more of the same" to contend with.

What's more, we now live in a time when no amount of "specialness" can insulate anyone from the adverse consequences of unguided human activity. It used to be that special interests were more or less safe from threats. The king stayed in his castle while his knights rode to the battlefield. The owner of a mining company wasn't afflicted by black lung himself. But as we've seen throughout this book, the nature of the threats today has changed. The playing field is leveled. A nuclear explosion will not pause at the door of the White House. And if global pollution renders our land inhospitable and our air unbreathable, no amount of money or power will shield any individuals or nations from the consequences. We're all in the same boat now, no matter what our special interest, and we must work together to change what must be changed when "more of the same" threatens our collective survival.

Our enemies will never agree.

    First, who are our enemies? Today the United States is at war in Afghanistan. So perhaps we could say unequivocally that our enemy is the Taliban. But a little less than thirty years ago, the Taliban was at war with the former Soviet Union—which was, at the time, an enemy to the United States. To help the Taliban defeat our enemy, we armed them. Then the Soviet Union fell, Russia rose as our tenuous friend, and today the Taliban fights US soldiers using the very weaponry the US government once handed them, free of charge. This same cycle has happened again and again in history. The United States was once willing to drop atomic bombs on the citizens of Japan; today they are considered our friends. Can you imagine Germany invading Poland or France today? The European Union has rendered that idea ridiculous—but it was possible less than a lifetime ago.

    And even if we could name our enemies with any certainty or permanency, how do we know they would never cooperate? Have we asked them? Imagine a United States citizens' movement that led to our political and religious leaders coming forward and declaring, "We are willing and ready to cooperate as equals among equals to seek an intelligent alternative to weaponry, to create a sustainable relationship with the environment, and to begin working toward the resolution of human injustice." Imagine then that our allies and friends—say, Britain, France, Japan, Canada, and Brazil—came forward and said, "Well, if you are, we are." Pretty soon more countries would join, perhaps countries with which we have only a tenuous partnership. Perhaps Russia, India, and China might cooperate. Eventually, you'd have a joint effort among the world's most powerful nations. The world's less powerful nations would have every incentive to follow suit—they could only benefit from a global effort to give the citizens of every nation an equal voice. So what if we then, collectively, turned to our current "enemies," those countries with which we have limited, strained, or no diplomatic ties? What if we said, "Iran, Afghanistan, and North Korea, are you in?"

Now imagine if they said no. They would be doing so on a global stage, with the citizens of every nation as an audience. When we turn to them and say, "Why would you prefer to continue to use weaponry rather than cooperating with us *as equals* to find an alternative?" . . . they would have to answer the question with the world listening.

And what if they came up with a valid reason? Then the onus would be on us to address their concerns and take another step toward our goal. But we'll never know their objections to our invitation to join us if we don't invite them in the first place. And perhaps they wouldn't have any objections at all. Perhaps they're just as tired of the ongoing killing, environmental destruction, and human suffering as we are. Perhaps if we extend the invitation, for the first time in history, the answer, from every corner of the globe, might be a unanimous, "Yes."

The American people will never be ready for this kind of change.

A few years ago, I was invited to Middlebury College to meet with James Martin, who, in 1978, wrote a book called *The Wired Society*. His book predicted exactly what has come to be in our culture—technologies like mobile phones, the Internet, electronic mail, and all the ways those technologies have changed interpersonal communications. He foresaw the future, and so he has been labeled a visionary.

When I sat down to discuss the idea for reorganizing ourselves on the macro level with him, his response was, "Forget it. The American citizen will never endorse this idea."

At first I was taken aback. There I was, with no credentials other than being an American citizen, and I had endorsed it. And I had also talked to numerous other average American citizens who were telling me that they would support this idea if it became an option.

Ironically enough, one of the objections I kept hearing from those citizens was, "Forget it. Our leaders will never endorse this idea."

Again and again, from all sides of the table, I've heard, "I agree. But *they* won't." I believe the idea I'm sharing is a workable, common sense solution to the global problems we all face—and maybe there are even better solutions out there. But we need to pick one. The time we once had in abundance to debate our future is running out. Just as I once worked to have the idea for a bike path bridge brought to the table, all I am asking now is that we not preemptively exclude this idea. Let's put it on the table, and before we say it will never be accepted, let's ask each other how we feel about it. And then let's ask the citizens of every other nation for their thoughts.

If this is such a good idea, why haven't our leaders endorsed it?

Many people have wondered why I am focusing my energies on the American people rather than American leaders. Since the inception of the Global Plan Initiative and later Globalsummit.org, I have at a few points reached out to our politicians. After writing *We Need a Plan*, I sent a copy to numerous national leaders in addition to many thinkers, diplomats, and philanthropists. I got very few responses, none of which came from our national leadership. And again, after President Barack Obama's election, I sent a letter to him and copied every US senator, congressperson, and the ambassadors from every nation with an embassy in the

United States. This time I received only one response from an American politician, a congressperson who, by policy, grants an interview to every citizen who requests one. The interview proved to be a brief, routine meeting with a member of his staff.

We cannot hope for change to be initiated by those invested in our status quo. Our current political leaders—however ethical and committed they might be—have devoted their personal lives to the world's existing tools for solving problems. It's unlikely that, given that kind of investment, they will be particularly motivated to talk about the possibility of creating new tools. Once this idea is a major part of public conversation, I think our leaders will find that it's in their best interest, too. But they won't be the catalyst. Though we will need our leaders' cooperation, the onus is on us, the American people, to initiate the process.

I'm not the one to blame. It's the Democrats, the Republicans, the terrorists, the big business executives, the communists, etc. that are causing the problems. Talk to them.

Blame does not create a solution. Even if we could achieve the impossible and unanimously agree on a single party, nation, or religious group that is to blame for the world's problems . . . would we be any closer to resolving those problems? My answer to this objection is the same as my answer to the objections stating, "special interest groups, our enemies, our citizens, or our leaders will never agree." When we point the finger of blame, we provide ourselves with a convenient psychological escape.

There are already organizations in place dealing with issues of peace, sustainability, and human injustice. Why not let them do their job?

Google the words "peace organizations" and you'll get well over twenty million hits. And still, there are at least twenty-five

Don't Drink the Water

ongoing, deadly armed conflicts taking place in the world as you read this chapter. And our leaders are now using a phrase we've never heard before: "perpetual war."

Google the words "environmental organizations" and you'll get thirty million hits. But the amount of toxic waste generated by human activity will be more today than it was yesterday and more tomorrow than it is today. And our list of environmental woes continues to grow—from overflowing landfills to soaring rates of childhood asthma.

"Social injustice organizations"? Seven million five hundred thousand hits. And yet at least 80 percent of humanity lives on less than ten dollars a day; UNESCO estimates that the world illiteracy rate is as high as 20 percent; and thirty thousand children died today from a preventable cause. Tomorrow, another thirty thousand children will be gone.

When I first began visiting different activist groups to talk about the need for a global plan, I found that I kept hearing the question, "Why don't you find an existing organization to support? Why reinvent the wheel?" So I searched. The only one that I was able to find that was really trying to look down the road in a practical way rather than reacting to an existing problem was the World Federalist Association. But even that organization, as I have explained before, seemed to me to be lacking key pieces of the puzzle. Ultimately, the result of my search was that I ended up on the mailing lists of hundreds of non-governmental organizations, each striving to confront one of the symptoms of a chronically ill species.

For just one month, I began collecting solicitation letters from those organizations. And at my next speaking engagement, I brought them along. I had two shopping bags full. I dumped them out on the table and asked simply, "Is this a workable plan for fixing what our governments leave for us to address?"

I mean no disparagement to the many individuals involved in these organizations, as workers in the field, support staff, and contributors. They all have my respect. But as a businessman I understand that it's impossible to solve our problems using this piecemeal approach. All of these individuals involved in working toward peace, sustainability, and justice are highly informed and highly qualified—but we're wasting their time by not providing them with an overarching system so that they can join forces and collaborate.

Yes, there are already organizations in place—and that means that we won't be starting from scratch. We've already got the personnel; we're already paying their salaries with our taxes and donations. Now let's help these individuals work smarter and more effectively by getting ourselves organized.

This sounds like a job for the UN.

Founding the United Nations was a noble and significant attempt at the kind of global, long-term thinking I'm advocating. But the UN was also founded based on the local, short-term values of nationalism. Its charter was written with intentional loopholes so that nations could choose to cooperate—or choose not to, with no penalty.

Imagine if, when the Constitution was written, our Founding Fathers had given five states veto power over any decisions made by congress. We'd be living in a very different nation. New York or California or Texas or some other large state might rise as a superpower, able to dictate the successes and failures of the other forty-nine states.

This is exactly the kind of power that the five permanent members of the UN Security Council—the United States, Russia,

Britain, France, and China—have today.

The United Nations was a first attempt. We owe our children an updated version.

Do we have the legal and diplomatic intelligence to make this idea a reality?

I heard this question often enough that eventually I decided to seek an answer from legal scholars. When I began looking for an individual to talk to who might be considered one of our nation's preeminent authorities in international law, more than one activist and thinker pointed me in the direction of Edith Brown Weiss. She is a highly regarded professor of international law at Georgetown University, and for five years, she sat on the three-person Inspection Panel of the World Bank. If any nation or group of individuals had an objection to a World Bank policy, they were able to appear before the panel for a fair and impartial hearing.

When I asked her if she thought we currently have the legal capacity to reorganize human activity, her answer was yes. But she added a stipulation: "No one will ever know for sure until we try it on a large enough scale."

The fact is that our legal and diplomatic minds are already working on this issue—and have been for decades, since the world wars first began to awaken humanity to the growing threats of nationalism. In 2002, 111 nations came together to form the International Criminal Court, another stepping stone on the path to an enforceable alternative to weaponry. The trouble with the ICC is that it only has the capacity to try individuals for a crime *after the fact*. First, someone must be accused of genocide, crimes against humanity, war crimes, or a crime of aggression; *then* the ICC can decide guilt or innocence. But the ICC cannot, as our Supreme Court can, mediate in disputes. Still, our only tool for settling national and religious disputes when negotiation fails is weaponry. And as my father taught me long ago: tightening your grip on the wrong tool only exacerbates the problem you're trying to fix. We need a new tool.

Our world's legal minds are ready, but their intelligence will not be released until we ask them to think beyond the existing framework of sovereign nations. Until then, they will keep treating the symptoms with partial solutions like the ICC—while the disease rages on unchecked.

We'll get there eventually; we just need more time. Why rush things?

The time is now. This idea might, at any point in history, have made sense as a way of organizing human activity and ensuring peace—but we had neither a dire need for it nor the tools to realize it until very recently.

It would have been absurd for President Theodore Roosevelt to stand up in 1902 and declare his intent to land an American shuttle on the moon. The same goal would even have been absurd for President Harry S. Truman in 1952. But in 1962, the United States had the technology and the world was ready for the goal to be set. And so, when President John F. Kennedy said, "We choose to go to the moon," the citizens applauded.

Today, human technology has made us all eyewitnesses to war, environmental destruction, and human injustice. It has also provided us with the capacity to consider enormous amounts of data and to experience and explore our many cultural differences and our many human similarities. We can transmit information from Spain to New Zealand in nanoseconds. Our children participate in interactive, global classrooms. Our national leaders can communicate with each other in real time from their own offices, oceans apart.

The world hasn't been ready before now because we haven't

had the need or the tools until now. But now we have them both . . . and more and more individuals and groups are recognizing it. The citizens of Germany have already amended their constitution to allow for relinquishing some national sovereignty when it is for the benefit of all humans and the redistribution of power is shared equally by all nations. They are ready. They have stood alone for too long.

Waiting is causing us to lose precious time. Ask yourself, "Would our children be better off if we came up with a successful successor to the UN?" If your answer is yes, why deny them the chance to have peace and prosperity sooner rather than later?

* * *

When I first began to seriously consider and talk about the need for reorganizing humanity on the macro level, I hoped that someone would prove me wrong. I hoped that someone would come up with a logical, pragmatic objection to the idea. Not a fear-based objection. Not an objection that involves blame or finger-pointing. Not an objection based on cultural insecurities about human potential or personal insecurities about being "just one average citizen." But an ironclad, fact-based objection that would make me say, "Oh, I didn't think of that! Thank you. Now I can go home."

If someone would make that argument, I could forget this idea. I could go back to my local, short-term life. I could spend more time with my son and daughter; I could play more Frisbee; I could sit quietly and enjoy the view of the Potomac from my balcony. There's no need to spend time thinking about our potential once you accept that war, environmental destruction, and human injustice are facts of life that we all have to live with—forever.

But no one has made that argument. And over the course of a lifetime of work, I've come to believe that it doesn't exist.

There are understandable fears associated with this idea. These should not be swept under the rug or disparaged. But we cannot effectively address our fears if we use them as an excuse for inaction. If, instead, we face them together, if we examine them and discuss them, we'll have a shot at moving beyond them.

Yes, there's a chance that on the first try, we'll hit a dead end—but if we do, we'll know far more for the next attempt than what we know now. And on the other hand, there's the possibility of *not* hitting a dead end, the possibility of creating the next step in the evolution of human intelligence. By giving this a fair shot, we stand to lose so little . . . and we stand to gain so much.

Chapter Sixteen

Recent history suggests that military powers—regardless of ideology—will take constructive steps toward global security only if an energetic public, in many parts of the world, insists that together we subordinate the pursuit of national power and wealth to the call for human survival and dignity.
—Robert C. Johansen, World Policy Institute

Decades ago in India and Nepal, when tigers were labeled an "enemy to man" rather than an "endangered species," hunters designed a method that used the tigers' fear of the unknown to kill them. They would unfurl an immense funnel of white cloth with an open end perhaps three or four miles wide. Gradually, the funnel would taper down to a closed point where a hunter waited in a tree, steadying his rifle. Boys astride elephants would spread out in quarter-mile intervals across the funnel's open end and begin to ride slowly forward into the funnel, shouting and banging sticks.

When they heard this noise, the tigers lounging in the tall grasses would perk up their ears and look about. They could not identify or understand the sound, but they knew that it was out of place. As all living creatures will, they strove to return to the familiar. They moved away from the intruding noise, and thus they were driven ahead of the elephants into the funnel and then closer and closer to the waiting marksman.

The white cloth walls of the funnel were only about four feet tall—high enough to block the vision of a moving tiger, but low enough for it to easily spring over. But a tiger's fear of the unknown will keep it from leaping when it cannot see where it is going to land. And so, instead, each trapped tiger would march steadily forward toward certain death.

Today, we are acting like these hunted tigers. As we persist in justifying our current activities and accommodating the consequences, we march toward a hopeless future. Behind us, we hear the cries of the victims of war, we hear the testimony of our best scientists warning of the end result of environmental destruction, and we hear the pleas for help of those who suffer from poverty, hunger, illiteracy, and preventable disease. We know that this turmoil is out of place; we want to achieve quiet, peace, and prosperity. But rather than addressing the sound, we shut it out by trying, futilely, to move away from it. Like the tigers, we have the capability to save ourselves; we could "jump" over the perceived barrier of human experience. But we do not—because we cannot see where we will land.

In the previous chapter, we addressed the many concerns and objections citizens tend to raise about the idea of holding a global summit to plan our own future. We went through them step by step, and it is my hope that you now have a fairly clear understanding of what this idea would *not* look like. It would not be a blame game; it would not involve creating a single, dictatorial global government; it would not mean casting aside the concerns of hardworking citizens.

But what *would* it look like? If we jump, where will we land?

Here is the difficult, but critically important point: there is no answer to that question. So many individuals whom I've talked to about the idea of reorganizing humanity on the macro level so that we can work together to achieve our common goals have asked me, "How can I ever sign on to this idea if you can't tell me what it will look like?" But I am not asking you to sign on to a yet-to-be-created organizational structure for guiding human activity. I am asking you to sign on to *committing to an attempt to create that structure*.

Eight hundred years ago, a group of English barons gathered together to outline certain liberties of man—and ultimately, they set them down in the Magna Carta. Four hundred years later, representatives from the monarchies of many warring European factions gathered together to create a new political order based on the concept of sovereign nation states. They set the agreement they came to down in a series of treaties called the Peace of Westphalia, which for the first time established a firm concept of nationhood in Europe. Little more than a century later, a group of colonial Americans agreed to assert their three inalienable human rights and declare independence from the British monarchy, and they all signed their names to a document written by Thomas Jefferson called the Declaration of Independence. Many of the same men gathered again at the Constitutional Convention, where, as we have seen in the previous chapter, they again set down their rights and goals in a document that became the Constitution of the United States of America. Finally, only a little more than sixty years ago, the members of the United Nations gathered together to decide upon a "common standard of achievement for all peoples and all nations," which they set down in the Universal Declaration of Human Rights.

There is a clear progression in these documents. Each one was a stepping-stone—from declaring individual freedom, to declaring national freedom, to promoting the collaboration of states to ensure freedom, to promoting the collaboration of nations to ensure freedom. The borders created by each document encompass more and more humans, and the level of intelligence and compassion involved in their creation doubles and redoubles. But the sentiment behind each document has been essentially the same: to protect the inalienable rights of human beings so that we might live free from threat.

No one asked any of the English barons to agree to the Magna Carta before they had written it. No one demanded that the ruling parties meeting in Westphalia bind themselves to anything before the fact. Thomas Jefferson did not insist that his compatriots accept the Declaration before he put pen to paper. The American colonies were not required to unify before the Constitutional Convention was held. And, finally, the Universal Declaration of Human Rights was created with the contribution of representatives from every member nation of the UN and was not ratified by any of those nations until their citizens and representatives were satisfied.

I am now proposing that we continue the evolution of the world's documents, that we work together to outline a new set of rules that will work for all of humanity. But just as was true of all the documents preceding the one I'm suggesting, no one will be bound by its rules unless and until everyone agrees. And that is why I cannot show you this document yet. It will be the collaborative brainchild of a team of representatives made up of our best thinkers and strategists, and it will be born of the goals, concerns, objections, and needs they voice on our behalf. The plan they ultimately outline will be returned to the citizens of every nation for evaluation, and before it is ratified, it will undergo a process of revision and amendment. But before we get to the point of holding the document in our hands, we have to commit to its creation. We have to select a team of representatives. We have to task them with the job. Until then, we cannot and should not begin to predict what their suggestions might be.

I understand that starting the journey without an exact, clear picture of the destination in mind can be a daunting prospect. But we should be wary of shortcuts. Any existing group that hands us a pre-made plan, created without a process of contribution and consensus, and says, "Here is the answer," cannot possibly be offering a solution that takes everyone's perspective into account. Just as Krishnamurti once stood up to tell his would-be followers, "There are no gurus," we must today remember that no one knows the path ahead—we are all walking it and discovering it together. Yes, if we had a pre-made plan in hand, we would then have the advantage of being able to evaluate it from the beginning—but we would lose the far more valuable advantage of being able to contribute to the plan's creation.

And if we work together, we will have a far greater chance of success. General Douglas MacArthur, perhaps the most celebrated war strategist in American history, said at the end of his life:

> *Abolition of war is no longer an ethical question to be pondered solely by learned philosophers and ecclesiastics, but a hard core one for the decision of the masses whose survival is the issue. Many will tell you with mockery and ridicule that the abolition of war can only be a dream . . . that it is the vague imagining of a visionary. But we must go on or we will go under! We must have new thoughts, new ideas, and new concepts. We must break out of the straitjacket of the past. We must have sufficient imaginations and courage to translate the universal wish for peace—which is rapidly becoming a universal necessity—into actuality.*

Today we stand inside the funnel of human experience. Like

the hunted tigers, we are using our past experience as our guide. But unlike the tigers, we know where we are headed. A world that works for all humans is not part of our past experience, but that does not mean it will never exist. The only way any future generation will live in such a world is for the existing generation to stop drinking the water of human experience and to have the courage and the confidence in ourselves to jump without knowing exactly where we'll land.

We *do* have one powerful, valuable tool that the hunted tigers lacked. We have the human imagination. We are capable of imagining ourselves on the other side—on the day after our world representatives gather together and commit to the process of establishing and achieving our goals. Imagining is the first step. Until we can see it in our minds, we'll never see it before our eyes.

In this book, I have shared with you my personal story in the hopes, first, of connecting on a human level and, second, of exciting your imagination. I learned over the course of my life's journey to reconsider the collective potential of humanity, and I hope that you, too, will have drawn from these stories a new perspective on what we are all capable of achieving.

And perhaps you have recognized some of your own struggles and discoveries in mine. Together, we began with the insecurity of childhood, the need to look toward authority and cultural labels as guides for navigating the world. We passed through the process many of us go through as we come of age—stepping outside the cage of culture and beginning to search for our own answers. And, out of that quest for independence came a renewed quest for connection—from the discovery I had at the top of a tower crane that the world is small and borderless to my efforts on the town council to bring about change that would benefit the citizens of Vienna, despite the opposition of special interests.

Don't Drink the Water

My personal journey included the despair I felt when I saw the path ahead coming to a dead end. Where once I had been convinced that we human beings are capable of taking the next step in our own evolution, I suddenly wondered if we might be stuck in a perpetual status quo, preoccupied by the mistakes of the past and fearful of the growing uncertainty of what's to come. The thought that we might be forever caught in the inertia of the present was, as you have seen, devastating to me. And I believe that all of us feel that devastation on some level. We learn to accommodate it, but at the same time, we cannot help but internalize our collective suffering. Ultimately we wind up telling ourselves, "I'm just one person. One member of a fatally flawed species. There's nothing I can do."

The only way out of this quagmire is to engage one of our most powerful tools: the human imagination. There *is* a new possibility on the other side of the funnel of human experience, and though we cannot see it, we can envision it. This book has been about examining our past and what we can learn from it, but far more importantly, it is about facing our future. It is about each one of us allowing the idea of a secure, sustainable, and reorganized world to capture our imaginations. And it is about, as Margaret Mead said, having the vision to "never doubt that a small group of thoughtful, committed citizens can change the world. Indeed, it's the only thing that ever has."

A few years ago, I was driving in Maine, and I happened to pick up an elderly hitchhiker named Milburn Templeton. He was a poet. In one of his poems that he shared with me, he wrote that words, when they do not capture our hearts, minds, and imaginations, are "dead spores caught in an updraft." And that is all this book is without you and your capacity to imagine. It is just a story. It is now our responsibility, together, to have the courage to translate this book from story into reality.

Victor Hugo wrote, "There is one thing stronger than all the armies in the world, and that is an idea whose time has come." The time has come for this idea. We now have the need and the tools to work together to intelligently design our own future. Once this idea is released into the world, there will be no containing it. It will spread, and in its spreading, eventually it will come to be.

But the onus is on us to start the chain reaction. If you have read this far, then I ask you to join me in taking the next step. First, allow this idea to ignite your imagination:

What if a citizens' movement led to the declaration of a global ceasefire, during which world representatives could prepare for and hold a global summit where the topic would be the long-term health of the entire human race?

Then talk about the idea of a global summit. Consider its potential—but this time, do so in cooperation with others. Ask each other what the world would look like without the lens of labels distorting our vision or the escape of accommodation distorting our thinking. Ask each other whether a global summit, held to establish goals for humanity's future and to reorganize human activity accordingly, has the potential to render accommodation obsolete. And ask each other for different suggestions, too. A global summit is one way to move us toward security and sustainability—but are there other ideas? If so, let's put them all on the table . . . and then pick one.

This book is not a call for volunteers or a request for donations. In fact, I am not asking you to change anything you do on a daily basis. I'm simply asking you to *allow this idea to become a part of the conversations you are already having.* We all have some ability to influence others, and we do it constantly, every time we come across a new idea that excites us. We tell our friends, "I loved this movie—you should see it!" We say to our parents, "I think you'd feel safer if you bought a cell phone to carry with you." We ask our neighbors, "Which cable company did you choose?"

Every day, in ways both big and small, we're asking each other for input and offering each other suggestions on improving our daily lives. We're sharing our successes and possibilities. And, we're dealing with a multitude of concerns already vying for our attention. I don't ask that you ignore any of your current joys or fears in favor of this one. But it is possible that this idea might encompass those joys and fears . . . so, if you're talking already, why not include this in the conversation?

If you are a parent, a teacher, a medical professional, or a church leader—someone who, in some capacity, teaches others every day—bring this idea into your discussions. If finding solutions for our world on both a local and global scale is already your forte as a teacher and leader, this idea could use your compassion and energy.

If you are a member of a church or social group, bring this idea into your conversations with other members. Find out just how compatible a movement for humanity's long-term health might be with your organization's short-term mission.

If you give to charitable organizations working on the world's current problems, from war to pollution to hunger, ask your organization's leadership to join the discussion, too. If you belong to a "Without Borders" network or an online network such as the True Majority or Avaaz, you are particularly well-situated to talk about global solutions. Send your organization a message. Let them know that as a member eager to see the organization's mission accomplished, you support a growing citizens' movement to reorganize humanity on the macro level. Ask them to propose the idea to their other members and supporters. Ask for their organizational endorsement. Talk to artists and academics. Talk to journalists. Talk to community organizers. Talk to public relations representatives, marketers, designers. Talk to people who, once they have allowed this idea to capture their imaginations, might be able to apply their unique talents and experience to helping it grow.

And reach out to individuals you might know or have some connection to who have a broader audience. Some of us have the ears of our families and close friends; some of us have wider circles of acquaintances and colleagues; and some of us, like politicians and celebrities, hold very large microphones.

We have the avenue of direct appeal to our political representatives, so if you feel so moved, write to your state politicians, your senators and congresspeople, and our president. Though as politicians they have a personal investment in the status quo, as human beings they have a much greater stake in the future of our world. So tell them so. Suggest to them that they join you in endorsing this idea.

But the political platform is only one avenue among many for spreading this idea. Our communications technologies and our culture have forever changed our modes of influencing human thought. Yes, we can talk to politicians, but imagine if Oprah, Bono, or Bill Gates endorsed this idea. So many celebrities, athletes, actors, and cultural figures are already using their extraordinary stature and wealth to work on the world's problems. They have the willingness, and they have the resources. Let's get them involved, too.

But, most importantly, keep this idea alive in your own imagination. Keep reimagining your potential and *our* potential. Keep returning to a different vision of the world, free from accommodation. Keep seeing what's possible in your mind, and soon enough, we'll all see it with our own eyes.

Years ago, as a boy, I sat with Mr. Steinhelper on his front porch, talking over the large and the small—just as we have done in this book. On one of those afternoons, I might have been complaining about some struggle at school or with my friends . . . the exact problem is now lost in my memory. But I do know that I was dealing with that ever-resurfacing, apparently insurmountable insecurity: "I'm just one person. There's nothing I can do."

Mr. Steinhelper turned to me and said, "Bobby, there's a saying I like. *If it is to be, it is up to me.*"

Today I would change one word of Mr. Steinhelper's advice.

If it is to be, it is up to *us*.

Acknowledgments

This book has been a lifetime in the making, and over the years, my efforts have been buoyed by both the direct and indirect support of many individuals. In a sense, my thoughts have been building toward the writing of this book since I was a child, and so my first acknowledgments must be to my sisters Linda and Paulette McCormick. They have nurtured, challenged, and accepted me from the beginning, and their love helped create the mental space I needed to research and reflect.

Although he appears in the pages of this book, I want to again emphasize the profound influence Mr. Steinhelper had on my life and thinking. Without his friendship, the boy I was could not have become the man I am, and this book would not exist. J. Krishnamurti is in the same category in my mind. Although we never met, his clarity of thought provided the template for my own questioning and thus the seed for this book.

Many friends, colleagues, and collaborators have walked beside me for all or part of the journey of Globalsummit.org. I wish to specially acknowledge Paul Sherrington, Lois McCormick, Roberta McDonald, Ruth Korobov, Neville Williams, Claire

Liston, Lyn Vencus, Carla Barzetti and Eileen Taylor-Harwood.

Teresa Spencer and I simply sat and talked, and from those conversations together we wrote a story I could never have written working alone. She was joined by Bree Barton, Kaytie Morris, and Peter Honsberger in providing the professional support I needed to turn research and discussion into words on the page.

My children Ben and Greta McCormick have listened to and loved me through the whole of this project. Their support has been essential.

The children I have met throughout my lifetime have provided the motivation I needed to write this book. I am especially grateful to Andrew, Michael, Katie, Zach, Piper, Ryan, Jack, Lucy, and Gage.

Breinigsville, PA USA
29 March 2011
258622BV00001B/10/P